POWERBIKES

POWERBIKES

LAURIE CADDELL

BLANDFORD PRESS

Poole   Dorset

First published in the U.K. 1981

Copyright © 1981 Blandford Press Ltd,
Link House, West Street,
Poole, Dorset, BH15 1LL

British Library Cataloguing in Publication Data

Caddell, Laurie
  Powerbikes.
  1. Motorcycles
  I. Title
  629.22′ 75   TL440

ISBN 0 7137 1021 7

Typeset by Poole Typesetting Ltd.
Colour reproduction Sackville Press, Billericay.

Printed in Singapore.

CONTENTS

INTRODUCTION

When I set about choosing thirty bikes for inclusion in *Powerbikes,* I tried to imagine someone finding a copy of the book tucked away in a corner of an antique bookshop a hundred years from now. I wanted the book to give an account of the machines, available in the late 1970s, not the small mopeds or learner bikes, but the fastest roadsters, the most powerful mud-pluggers and the swiftest racers. It had to be a document on the state of the art in the middle to late twentieth century, and had to convey how hard or easy they were to live with as well as ride. I doubt whether Powerbikes will be with us for many more decades, even if fuel does hold out, for every year more stringent pollution and safety regulations come into force which indirectly single out the motorcyclist and his pleasure machine and set him apart from the rest of the automotive world. They will say that cars are necessary because most people can drive, but Powerbikes are a specialised form of transport and we can't have people buying fossil fuels so they can enjoy themselves when others need it to get to work. Looking at it from the other side, it is not too depressing, for if you treat every day as your last day of being allowed to ride a bike, you will enjoy every minute of riding twice as much!

From the very first days, the motorcyclist has been a breed apart from the car driver and, as time has modified and automated the four-wheeler, so the gulf has opened up between the two factions: bikes are still as primitive to ride as ever and that is the best part of the fun. From the very first days, too, there has been a slow but steady upping of performance with bikes both on the track and off, so that now we have a whole pocketful of Powerbikes, priced from as little as £1,000 for a big off-roader to £10,000 for a circuit-racer capable of carrying its rider to World Championship honours.

The history of motorcycling has had its fair share of Powerbikes, however, with the first practical four-cylinder machine being the 1904 FN, built by the famous Belgian arms company. With such features as a five-main-bearing crankshaft and shaft final drive, the 412cc could be mistaken in specification almost for a machine of today. Only its 3½ hp output and 35 mph top speed would give the game away. America was soon to follow Belgium's lead and they produced several multis in the 1910s and 1920s, with such famous names as Cleveland, Henderson, Pierce and Ace. England has had

'multis' too, with the Ariel square fours, which started life as 500s and grew to full 1-litre bikes, while the Italians eclipsed everybody with the 500cc Moto Guzzi V8 of 1957, surely the most 'cylindered' bike we are ever likely to see.

There seem to be few signs of the power race dying down as yet, for, even after planning, this book has missed out on several later additions. For instance, Suzuki have introduced a new top-of-the-range bike, the GSX1100 with four valves per cylinder, futuristic instrumentation and more power than they care to admit to, while Honda have brought out a version of their CB900 with a ten-speed transmission, and we can only be thankful that, for peace of mind and conservation of our roads, the bike has to be stopped before the upper five ratios can be selected. What of the NR500 Honda racer? Of V4 design, the four-stroke engine features four camshafts, eight sparking plugs, oval cylinders and thirty-two valves, with an estimated power output of 120 bhp. Honda only race so that they can milk their circuit technology and employ it in their roadsters, so from that point of view the future looks rosy for the technology-hungry Powerbike rider of the 1980s.

The machines I have included in the book virtually choose themselves, as they are, in every case, the best in each of their classes. There is tremendous rivalry between all the Japanese manufacturers and has been since 1968 when Honda announced their 750-four and so beat Kawasaki to the line in the first round of the revived power race. With every new top-line model emanating from either Yamaha, Suzuki, Honda or Kawasaki, you can bet that the rest will be watching closely to see if the new model in the vast arena will show up any areas of technological progression that the others have missed and, basically, if it is faster and more powerful than their own. The chances are that every model produced will be better and quicker than everybody else's and so the vicious circle spirals upwards, waiting for the next would-be king.

In Italy, finance dictates that things will happen more sedately, with Moto Guzzi, Benelli, Ducati and Laverda spending their time and money on honing their already established bikes, with the great new model only appearing once every few years. Even so, the Latin machines are never far behind their Oriental counterparts in terms of outright performance and they always make up on the roundabouts what they lose on the swings with their fine handling. Spare a thought for MV-Agusta, however, who have recently disappeared from the market and so taken from us one of the finest big bikes of modern times, the 140 mph Monza. In all my years of motorcycling, the Monza appealed to me as the ideal Powerbike, with its typical Italian fine handling and its 90 bhp twin-cam four-cylinder powerhouse engine. Whenever one is asked to imagine the perfect bike, the answer always seems to lie in the Italian chassis/Japanese engine region, forgetting that the fire-engine red MVs from Northern Italy already had the best of both worlds, even if the end result did cost £5,000. Reliable Japanese engines are very nice and very easy to live with, but somehow come nowhere near to the sound and feel of the two-wheeler equivalent to the Ferrari. I have included the MV because no work on the big bikes of the late 1970s should omit it, even if only to jog those with enough money to get the company on its feet again.

For an off-road bike, the Honda XL500S would have to grace my stable as it so neatly combines the roles of powerful roadster and serious mud-plugger that any other bike would only detract from either category. Any machine which can hit 90 mph, on tarmac or off, just has to be taken seriously and the fact that its manners are exemplary is a bonus. Counterbalanced engine, automatic engine decompressor and superb tyres equally suitable for all conditions make the Honda an easy bike to live with. It is all worthwhile when, after a hard day's trail, you can ride straight home and yet be able to out-corner some so-called 'sporting' machinery on the highways.

To complete my collection, I would have an RG500 Suzuki purely for toying with on the race track, if you can 'toy' with such an impeccable piece of engineering. It is nice to know that your bike can turn a 9 sec ¼ mile and gallop on to 180 mph if you really want it to; that it can be banked to 47° to pull about 1.3 g if your nerves and knees can stand the strain; and that it can just about flip over forwards if you pulled the brake lever hard enough. Yes, it is a nice feeling knowing that a bike has so much in hand . . . .

Even though I have taken just one bike from each of the three categories in this book for 'my'

collection, it shouldn't detract from the other models. I would have a fully faired Gold Wing for those long motorway trips; a Bimota for when the MV was unwell; a CBX to impress the neighbours; a Quasar to win friends and influence people and a Harley-Davidson because it is a Harley-Davidson. Each has its own niche in the market and each, however similar it may appear to be to a rival, has its own character and own brand of power. The quest for power will have to stop sooner or later as oil runs out and safety regulations come in, so I feel privileged to have been able to ride these bikes already and just hope that a few more come my way. While the petrol is there and the legislation isn't, go out and buy a big bike now, for whether you are a budding Sheene, Noyce or just plain John Smith road-burning superstar, all that power is a mere twistgrip away. Enjoy it while you still can.

Laurie Caddell October 1979

Conversion Table

1 lb = 0.454 kg
1 pt = 0.568 l
1 gal (UK) = 4.544 l
1 cu in = 16.387 cc
1 in = 2.54 cm = 25.4 mm
¼ mile = 400 m
1 mile = 1.609 km
1 mph = 1.609 km/hr
1 mpg (UK) = 0.354 km/l = 282.5 l/100 km
1 psi (lb/sq in) = 0.0703 kg/sq cm
1 lb ft = 0.1382 kg/m
1 hp = 0.746 kW

HONDA MT125R

The Honda MT125R made its first public appearance at the Earl's Court Show during the autumn of 1976. At that time it was announced that a batch of thirty-five of these machines was due to arrive in Britain at the beginning of the following year. The idea was to sell the bikes at cost price to selected dealers in the trade and they would nominate and support a rider of their choice. Each machine would compete in the Honda 125 Championship, with eight rounds, taking place at various international events during the 1977 season. As an incentive, the prize money offered at each race was £200 for a win and, at the end of the series, the overall winner would receive £1,000. With this type of formula it was obvious that the resulting races would be exciting and everything rested on the riders' skill and ability. The only specification changes allowed were to the riding position, chains, sprockets, tyres and sparking plugs.

The first round took place at Oulton Park, West Yorkshire, England, on Easter Monday 1977 and it was generally accepted as being a great success. Up to this time 125-class racing had been gradually deteriorating. This was mainly due to lack of spectator interest, but, once the Honda 125 Championship got under way, the revival of the class was greatly received by one and all. In fact the series was so successful that Honda have run the Championship ever since, and it is still as popular as in 1977.

The power unit of the little Honda is basically the same as that belonging to their CR125 motocross bike. It is an air-cooled, single-cylinder, two-stroke engine that is claimed to produce 26 bhp at 10,500 rpm. Maximum torque is developed at the same revs and this perhaps indicates a rather narrow power band.

Internally the motor has some interesting modifications over its motocross cousin. Although the bottom end is fairly ordinary, the barrel is unusual in that it is retained by its own set of studs. The cylinder head is then fixed by another set, whilst the whole arrangement discourages the studs from stretching.

The little Honda MT125R around which the Honda 125 Championship is based. All the bikes in the series are identical, so the winner of each race is obviously the best rider.

The single-cylinder, two-stroke engine which nestles in the Honda's frame.

When examining the barrel, one is confronted by a maze of overlapping ports. There are the usual four transfer ports and a rectangular inlet port that is bridged in order to support the piston rings. The remaining exhaust port is unusual in that it is L-shaped but, apart from these, Honda have added an extra transfer port just above the inlet. This increases engine efficiency during the period when the fresh mixture is being drawn in. As well as the inlet, the exhaust port is also bridged and Honda technicians found it necessary to drill two small lubrication holes in the piston skirt. This reduces the possibility of overheating and eventual seizure that could occur along the exhaust bridge. The rest of the system is quite conventional. Mixture is

drawn in through a Mikuni carburettor, while the exhaust system is of the usual expansion chamber design.

The frame chosen by Honda is of the semi-cradle design. It has a single front downtube and a wide diameter spine, with smaller tubes supporting the engine and the rear section. A conventional swinging arm is used and this operates in conjunction with a pair of heavy-duty rebuildable dampers. Front suspension is provided by telescopic forks.

On the track, the Honda performs with the

The MT125R has a conventional rear-end suspension set-up and as you can see everything is easy to get at.

enthusiasm of its 125cc four-stroke ancestor that
became so successful during the mid-1960s.
Although perhaps not as powerful, the MT125 is
perfect for the task for which it was designed and
competitive small-capacity racing can once again be
seen at circuits around the country.

Once the Honda has been started, the engine has
to be really revved and the clutch slipped in order to
get the bike moving. A close ratio six-speed gearbox
is used to keep the motor singing, and this is aided
by a wet multi-plate clutch situated on the right-
hand side. Gear changing is typically Honda and
selections can be made with the minimum of fuss.
Despite the high bottom gear, the bike is quite
capable of performing wheelies when accelerated
hard. This is mainly due to the low dry weight of

*Note how narrow the tank is, so that the rider can
grip it tightly with his knees and cut down on
aerodynamic drag, which is especially critical on such
a small racer.*

around 154 lb, which makes it feel more like a 50cc
than a 125cc machine.

The power comes in when the motor reaches
8,000 rpm, but it soon dies drastically once 11,000
rpm is passed. The motor must be kept within this
power band and preferably above 10,000 rpm. If the
revs are allowed to drop below 8,000 rpm, then the
motor will refuse to pull and, consequently, the bike
becomes totally unridable. In top gear, on a long
straight, the little Honda will easily exceed 100 mph
and no doubt this can be achieved on many of the
British circuits.

The steering is both light and positive, although

on bumpy stretches the bike tends to twitch slightly at high speeds. Fortunately, this does not happen when negotiating the bends, but with such a light machine the problem is hard to cure. Generally speaking the handling is very good and the bike will hold its line right through the corners without fear of drifting.

Braking is provided by a cable-operated single disc at the front and a similar stopper at the rear. The units strongly resemble those used on the Honda CB125T roadster, but on the track they proved more than adequate in slowing down this nimble machine.

Due to its relatively small dimensions, the MT125's riding position is rather cramped. Tall riders will find themselves unable to tuck down behind the screen and this could be a disadvantage when every ounce of speed is needed during a race. Nevertheless, the rider who is able to crouch down behind the screen will get a perfect view of the instrumentation. As on most racing machines, there is only a rev counter fitted and this one terminates at 13,000 rpm. It is doubtful though whether any rider will see more than about 11,250 rpm on the clock; if they do then something must be amiss!

The Honda has been definitely well designed. The stylish fairing and seat unit give the bike a purposeful look, which must aid high speed performance due to the streamlining effect. Overall, the bike is a neat little racer that is both simple in design and competitive on the track. No doubt its impressive performance, coupled with reliability and low cost, is why the Honda MT125R is a favourite with the clubmen and the championship contenders alike.

Light enough to pick up and throw around, but the Honda has enough power to give it a top speed of over 100 mph.

Engine: transversely mounted, single-cylinder two-stroke of 125cc with piston porting. Single carburettor. Maximum power 26 bhp at 10,500 rpm. Bump start.

Transmission: wet multi-plate clutch and six-speed gearbox. Chain final drive.

Frame and suspension: single downtube cradle frame with telescopic front fork and rear swinging arm with coil-spring/damper units.

Brakes: single disc front and drum brake rear.

Performance: maximum speed around 100 mph. Fuel consumption approximately 26 mpg.

KAWASAKI KR250/350

The world of motorcycle road-racing went mad in the early 1960s with the three major Japanese manufacturers using their own particular and unique technology to achieve success on the tracks. Multi-cylinder engines were used, whatever the capacity, and more and more gears were added to the bikes, with the smaller machines naturally having more ratios to keep their engines boiling in their smaller power bands. While the industry learned a great deal from these exploits, and the rivalry between teams intensified, with speeds always escalating, it meant that, for those without the lucrative works rides, it was hardly worth competing. Even if factory 125cc five-cylinder bikes and 250cc six-cylinder machines had been available to the average club rider, their costs would have been prohibitively expensive and who, without a mechanical genius and a good deal of luck, could strip down a twelve-speed gearbox?

Something had to be done and so the FIM (Fédération Internationale Motocycliste) banned machines over two cylinders in the smaller classes and restricted them to a mere six gears. Yamaha were, at this time (1970), getting into their stride with their production racing 250 and 350cc bikes which, as just about everybody who wanted to race had one, started to take World Championship titles. The machines were fairly basic two-stroke twin-cylinder-powered bikes and featured simple piston porting. Apart from a foray into the 250 and 350cc field by Harley-Davidson, which resulted in three Championships, Yamaha have continued to dominate the field. That was until the arrival of Kawasaki in early 1976.

Kawasaki's aim was to wrest the two Championships from Yamaha and to have their little 'green meanies' at the head of the field, even if the rest was still wholly Yamaha. Kork Ballington finally achieved the company's aims in 1978, with both crowns, and went on to repeat the dose in 1979. Both years he used the almost identical KR250 and KR350 bikes and both years there was little opposition, apart from his team-mate Gregg Hansford.

The company had a clean sheet of paper when it came to designing their racers and nothing was to be adopted from their roadsters, as had happened with their 500 and 750cc racing machines. The priorities were: disc valves, good power output, naturally, and compact shape for the adoption of streamlined

The twin Mikuni carburettors, which deliver fuel to the engine via the 'bacon slicer' disc valves.

bodywork. If they had used a parallel twin, like Yamaha, and had disc valves, that would have meant one carburettor either side and obviously that was no use for a bike with a small frontal area. The only option open seemed to be an in-line twin, mounted longitudinally in the frame, not with a longitudinal crankshaft, but with two crankshafts working in tandem. With that sorted, the rest of the bike could be built conventionally around that layout. As water-cooling was to be used, the problems of keeping the rear cylinder in the airstream was irrelevant.

Behind the fairing you can see the KR250's dry clutch. Note the superb contouring of the fuel tank.

The little 'green meanie' as campaigned very successfully by twice-250cc World Champion Kork Ballington.

The KR bikes use magnesium-alloy blocks with aluminium cylinders and the front cylinder is mounted slightly to the right of the rear, so that the necessarily large disc valves can be accommodated. Fibre discs are driven off the left-hand side of the crankshafts and breathing is through two Mikuni carburettors. When the bike was first used, it was a coupled 180° twin with one piston at top dead centre while the other was at the bottom. Although this gave a fairly smooth power delivery, vibration set in and made the bike uncomfortable, as well as prone to shaking itself to bits. It was then decided to make the simple step of having the pistons moving together; in effect to make the bike a twin-engined bike with two 125cc cylinders geared together. This cured the vibration problem and did not affect the power output at all. Incidentally, it is this that gives the Kawasakis their unique sound, a rather flat throaty drone as if they are either very sick or in a poor state of tune. The cylinder heads have large squish bands and give a compression ratio of 7:1 which is very high for a two-stroke machine. Mixture is blended on a 20:1 basis. The dimensions of the engine are 54×54 mm in 247cc form and 64×54 mm in 347cc form. The company do not quote actual power figures as their machines are not on sale to the general public, but they do say that the 250cc produces around 60 bhp at the crankshaft, while the larger machine produces nearer 75 bhp. The bikes both have useful power bands, with the 250s stretching between 9,000 rpm and 12,500 rpm, and the larger one staying on song between 8,500 rpm and 11,200 rpm. Drive is taken from the engine through a dry multi-plate clutch to a six-speed gearbox and thence by chain to the rear wheel.

The compact power unit sits in a narrow Duplex frame and is rubber-mounted at three points, further to cut out any vibration that might get through. Front suspension is of conventional design while the rear is similar to Kawasaki's Uni-Trak system, which has proved so effective on the company's motocross machines. Basically, it comprises a vertical spring/damper unit mounted just behind the gearbox with a rocker arm mounted just above and behind it. The rocker is connected on the other side by two rods which go downwards either side to the box-section swinging arm. As well as being adjustable on the units themselves, the geometry can be altered fairly simply on the rocker so that different rates can be used. Also, the system

is more compact than a conventional monoshock unit and does not need area above the engine, so that the whole bike can be shorter and again present a small frontal area to the wind. A variety of different wheels and tyres and brakes have been fitted to the works' bikes of several Kawasaki distributors, but Ballington has succeeded with single discs either end on both bikes, the front being larger than the rear and substantially cross-drilled to save weight. His bikes have been fitted with Campagnolo wheels and Dunlop tyres.

Cross-drill any more from this disc brake and you won't have any brake left at all. Little things like that, however, mean the difference between a World Championship and the obscurity of second place.

The tail fairing hides the Uni-Trak suspension but cannot obscure that purposeful-looking, box-section swinging arm.

A great deal of work has gone into the aerodynamics of the little racers and careful plumbing has been used on the exhaust systems, with the front cylinder exiting from the right side and sweeping directly under the frame and out under the left side by the swinging arm; the rear cylinder exhausts straight back and then inside the rider's leg to terminate above the rear wheel, way back past the saddle. This permits a shallow fairing with a lot of ground clearance which can be tapered at the front lower edge to penetrate the air. The drag coefficient of the 350cc bike was recently checked in a wind tunnel and found to be 0.470 Cx which, although not brilliant is respectable. What this does mean is that an awful lot of power is consumed just cutting the bike and rider through the air, without thinking about acceleration. It was then worked out how much power was needed to drive the bike and rider through still air at certain speeds and the figures were given as 14.8 bhp at 91.5 mph; 33.2 bhp at 122 mph and a whopping 56 bhp at 146 mph. When one considers that quite a lot of the power doesn't reach the back wheel, and that power around 70 bhp does, then a great chunk is taken just holding the bike at a constant speed, without the machine trying to accelerate. In spite of the drag, the bikes are still astonishingly quick for their capacities, with around 160 mph being possible on the larger machine and 10-12 mph less on the 250cc. With gearing to take them to such velocities, the standing start acceleration is not impressive, and it is a fair bet that road-going bikes of similar capacity could beat them away from standstill to around 50 mph. Once about 6,000 rpm has been reached on the racers, however, there will be no stopping them, providing the rider can keep the front wheel of the 230 lb bikes on the floor and not waste the power by having them paw at the air.

Fuel consumption is hardly of any importance when it comes to racing, but the smaller model can cover around 115 miles on a 5.1 gal tankful, making its consumption around 22 mpg, while the 350 returns just over 20 mpg. All in all, the little 'green meanies' have earned a great deal of praise from all of their riders, with their excellent low-speed acceleration and fine handling being the biggest plus points. They have always sounded the slowest bikes on the course and their riders, Ballington in particular, often look very slow, but in the past two years, they have been beaten to the flag on very few occasions indeed.

With both needles of the dials straight up, water temperature will be 80°C and revs 12,000; maximum performance should ensue . . .

Engine: longitudinally mounted with transverse twin-cylinders, two-stroke of 247 and 347cc. Disc valve induction. Two carburettors. Maximum power 60 bhp and 75 bhp at the crankshaft, respectively. Bump start.

Transmission: dry multi-plate clutch and six-speed gearbox. Chain final drive.

Frame and suspension: Duplex cradle with telescopic front fork and swinging arm with single upright coil-spring/damper unit, operated by rocker.

Brakes: single disc front and single disc rear.

Performance: maximum speed approximately 148 mph and 160 mph, respectively, and depending on gearing. Fuel consumption approximately 22 mpg and 20 mpg respectively.

SUZUKI SP370

Suzuki is no stranger to the off-road riding scene. Between them, works Suzuki team riders, Joel Robert and Roger DeCoster, have grabbed world motocross titles for the Japanese company by the bagful. The works Suzuki motocross machines are, of course, thoroughbred two-stroke screamers, so it comes as something of a surprise to find Suzuki marketing a bike like their SP370.

For a start the SP370 is not a motocross machine. In fact it is not even an enduro model. It is a docile dual purpose street/off-road bike. Secondly, the SP370's engine is a single-cylinder, four-stroke unit, a good old-fashioned powerplant in the mould of the pre-war British thumpers.

From initial observations it would appear that the bike was intended as a direct rival to Yamaha's four-stroke XT500. Suzuki, however, seemingly not wishing to tackle the rival XT500 head on, have chosen to go a different route with their SP370, offering a bike that is lighter, smaller and less expensive than the Yamaha. In this way, they probably hoped to attract the kind of rider who could be interested in a four-stroke off-road machine but felt that the thundering XT500 would be just too much to contemplate. The fact that the SP370 now sells in large numbers, particularly in the United States, must surely be proof that Suzuki's original thinking was sound. There are, after all, not many riders around who can really stretch a thundering XT500 to its limits on a fast and slippery dirt trail.

The power unit of the SP370 is a single-cylinder unit, utilising a single overhead camshaft and measuring 369cc. The engine breathes through a single 32 mm Mikuni carburettor and, with a compression ratio of 8.9:1, pushes out a claimed 25 bhp at 7,500 rpm. Engine lubrication is by means of the wet sump system while the ignition is by contact breaker and coil, the power for the spark being supplied by a 6 V battery.

The SP370's frame is of the usual tubular cradle type with a single front downtube. Front suspension is by means of a telescopic fork, while the rear end is catered for by a swinging arm and adjustable coil-spring dampers in conventional position. The front wheel is 21 in in diameter while the rear wheel measures 18 in.

The SP370's transmission features a five-speed gearbox with final drive, naturally, by chain. The whole SP370 package is a visually attractive motor-

The large 'thumper' engine sits high up in the frame, out of harm's way, leaving the underside of the frame nice and smooth.

cycle that combines the practical features of an off-road bike with the comfort and style of a roadster.

The SP370's major strength is the fact that it is a true dual-purpose machine. It is big and comfortable enough to be ridden considerable distances on the road while it is also strong enough to take the bashing it gets on the rough. True it's no dirt racer but it is still enough to give most off-road riders plenty of thrills and good times.

On the road the SP370 presents itself as a competent, if not particularly quick, performer. It can chug along happily at 65 mph and, if really aroused, can reach a top speed of almost 85 mph.

The leading-link front fork gives plenty of travel on the SP400, thus making easy work of terrain like this.

A few engine modifications to the SP370 Suzuki took it up to the more usual 400cc bracket.

A conventional rear end for the Suzuki with rather too many solid protuberances which could easily be damaged in a tumble.

Because of the steady and reliable nature of its four-stroke motor, the owner can actually ride his bike to his favourite dirt patch rather than having to load it up on a trailer as he might have to do with many of the SP370's more exotic two-stroke rivals. In addition, the SP370 motor returns about 70 mpg — even more if ridden sedately — which, with a fuel tank that carries 2 gal, means a range in the region of 150 miles. That figure is not unreasonable even for many a true road bike. The bike is also very comfortable to ride on the road. The tyres offer excellent grip with little of the speed wobbling and sliding exhibited by a number of so-called off-road bikes. The bike is also very civilised in that it has direction indicators plus a thoroughly effective headlight. Rear-view mirrors are also available, which means that the owner can use the bike on the road without any qualms most of the time.

Come the weekend and the SP370 can be converted into a genuine off-road bike. The engine produces enough power to enable the bike to go almost anywhere the rider is capable of reaching. The advantage of a four-stroke engine is that it usually has plenty of low-down torque and the SP370 is no exception. It can be ridden at almost walking speed in any of the first three gears. The turning circle of the machine is not all it could be but the suspension is good enough to allow the bike to cope with even the most vicious of bumps and jumps. The engine ground clearance also leaves something to be desired but at least Suzuki have fitted a substantial sump guard to protect the bike's vulnerable underbelly. The sleek torque characteristics of the four-stroke engine allow for smooth take-offs, but, if there is a major complaint to be made of the SP370, it is that the transmission snatches during throttle run-off. Although there is a cush drive within the rear hub, throttle run-offs and roll-ons can produce a series of jerks which make smooth riding on dirt a difficult proposition. The problem is further aggravated by the fact that the high compression nature of the four-stroke engine makes for rather rapid slowing down during throttle run-offs anyway. Nevertheless, this jerky motion can be compensated for and is not enough to spoil an otherwise satisfactory ride. The SP370's main asset is its ability to pull its way out of almost any situation. Thick mud holds no terrors for the SP370 and neither does soft sand. The four-stroke motor simply churns its way through almost everything nature cares to throw at it.

For a bike which is so at home in the dirt, the SP370 is a most refined machine. For reasons of weight a starter motor is not fitted but the kickstart mechanism is an improvement light years ahead of the typical British bangers of years gone by. To start the machine, all the rider does is to look at the small window on top of the valve cover and then turn over the engine by prodding on the kickstart until a small chrome screw head appears in the window. At this stage the bike is ready to be kicked into life and it usually takes no more than a couple of kicks before the throaty exhaust note bursts into song.

For the rider who wants a bike on which he can commute to work, yet also use over the weekend for off-road riding, the SP370 is a sensible proposition. Its road manners are first-class. On the dirt it is, needless to say, not as good as many of its fulltime off-road rivals but it is an excellent compromise. You'd have to be a pretty fair off-road rider to claim that the SP370 was insufficient for your average weekend riding needs. If you are looking for a Baja racer forget the SP370; it was never meant to be that kind of bike. It could be modified into a racer but then its mild-mannered road characteristics would have to be sacrificed and, for a bike which is as pleasant to ride on all surfaces as the SP370, that would be a crying shame.

Engine: transversely mounted, single-cylinder four-stroke of 369cc with two valves per cylinder operated by a single overhead camshaft. Single 32 mm carburettor. Maximum power 25 bhp at 7,500 rpm. Kick start.

Transmission: wet multi-plate clutch and five-speed gearbox. Chain final drive.

Frame and suspension: Duplex cradle with telescopic front fork and rear swinging arm with coil-spring/damper units.

Brakes: drum front and rear.

Performance: maximum speed 85 mph, acceleration over a standing start 1/4 mile 15 sec. Fuel consumption 65 mpg.

HONDA XL500S

The 1970s have seen a great trend towards fun bikes, two-wheeled vehicles designed specifically for leisure activities off-road. Trail bikes became popular in all sizes, but it was soon apparent that there was a lot of potential for proper dual-purpose machines, ones which could be used as commuters during the week and as a handy off-road machine at the weekends. When Honda revived their range and produced the XL/S series, they

The Honda's power unit is a punchy ½-litre four-stroke with all the power you could wish for.

Honda's superb XL500S is as much at home on the highway as the byway and is a real high-performing dual-purpose machine.

showed that the seemingly impossible task of producing a bike that was excellent on either surface, rather than one which was merely adequate on both, could be achieved.

The top of the range is the XL500S, a 'thumper' in the true British tradition but given that spicing of Japanese ingenuity and reliability which makes it an easy machine to live with. As in most off-roaders, the Honda uses a single-cylinder engine, in this case of 497cc and very oversquare dimensions. A single overhead camshaft is used and this activates four valves per cylinder for more efficient breathing. A 32 mm carburettor is used, while there are two separate double-skinned exhaust pipes trailing from the cylinder head and winding, one either side, past the single-downtube frame. As you can imagine, a big single does not thrive on revs and will pull strongly from low engine speeds. This is indeed the case with the Honda, which produces 34 bhp at 6,250 rpm and maximum torque of just under 30 lb ft nearer 5,000 rpm; maximum engine speed is 7,250 rpm. Single-cylinder engines are of course very lumpy but Honda have gone a long way to try to cure this and have built two contra-rotating counterbalances into the unit which cancel out a lot of unwanted vibration. Although still very much a single-cylinder engine in power delivery, it is as smooth as some twins and quite comfortable to ride on the road.

Kicking a big single into life is not the easiest of jobs but, with a compression ratio of 8.6:1, the XL is not as difficult as many. On the similar SR500 Yamaha bike, there is a little window just over the camcase which indicates when top dead centre has been reached so that it is possible to ease the engine over compression and then kick hard. Other manufacturers use a decompressor which opens a

That long chain will get very mucky off-road so should be cleaned regularly to enhance its life.

valve in the head so that the pressure is released. Honda have gone one better than all the rest, however, and built in an automatic system which, as the kickstart is pushed down, releases a decompressor so that no fiddling with the hands is needed and strength and concentration can be directed solely at swinging the motor into life. Surprisingly, a great deal of force still has to be exerted and rarely will the engine catch on the first kick.

Drive from the engine goes through a wet multi-plate clutch (which features a cushioning spring to ease engagement and make pulling away smoother) to a five-speed gearbox and by chain to the rear wheel. Like the rear brake lever on the other side, the gear lever is very narrow and distant from the pegs; large boots are needed to reach it and, even then, unless your toes are angled in, it is sometimes easy to miss. The frame is of conventional design for an off-road bike and is of single-downtube design with a fairly high-mounted swinging arm. Honda use a conventional rear suspension with lay-down dampers giving a triangulated geometry and the design gives 7 in of travel; the front, set up with a leading axle, is raked at 28.5° and has a generous 8 in of movement. Honda have found with their very successful motocross machines that a 'penny-farthing' wheel arrangement is best and the XL500S follows this trend, with an enormous 23 in front wheel and an 18 in rear. Tyres are of special design with a block pattern for off-road work yet proper profiling so that they can be leaned into corners on smooth surfaces. Naturally, there is a compromise both ways, but the important thing is that, unless you are trying to be a Graham Noyce off-road, the tyres will be adequate and yet still afford a good amount of grip at average speeds on the road, something that other trailbike tyres cannot do (until their covers are worn flat that is).

Two small drum brakes are used and they really are not up to the job, for, although it is easy to lock the rear wheel by standing on the pedal, the front unit just cannot be made to work hard enough. Considering that the bike weighs just under 300 lb, that is a problem and just would not be tolerated on a roadster of such dimensions. This is the only serious defect the bike has, for, in all other respects, it performs well in both roles. The performance is excellent and the bike will pull away from standstill at an exceptional rate; so much so that a great deal of

Can you find a coil-spring/damper unit longer than this on a road-going bike? It certainly soaks up the bumps when the going gets rough.

care and effort has to be used to keep the front end on the ground and the sheer pull of the engine will pull the front wheel off the deck at speeds approaching 50 mph, whether the rider is aware of the matter or not. Top speed is quite astounding for such a bike and will be somewhere past 90 mph, with a standing start ¼ mile occupying just over 15 sec, which puts the XL in the quick roadster class.

Fuel consumption is something to write home about, too, for it will turn in over 50 mpg and a fair bit more if used exclusively on the road. Handling on tarmac is good and, for once, it is possible to corner at a high speed without worrying about the tyres letting go prematurely. Although they make a little noise about their work, they hang on and let fairly respectable angles of lean be built up. With a light-weight, this also helps the cornering power. On the rough, the bike is equally at home with good ground clearance (just over 10 in) and plenty of suspension travel to soak up all the ruts, gulleys and bumps which you are likely to come across.

Although geared for a high top speed, the XL has no trouble pulling up high gradients on rough ground and that is where a 0.5-litre dual-purpose machine comes into its own. However, if there is enough power to levitate the front wheel on the tarmac, there is more than enough to send the bike somersaulting backwards on uneven terrain and to upset the balance of machine and rider. In the right hands, it would be fair to say that the Honda has the capability of being a reasonable mount in small club scramble events but that also means that, in the wrong hands, ie those of little experience, rider and bike could soon end up damaged and yards apart.

For general day-to-day work, the bike comes complete with twin mirrors, indicators, a neat speedometer with total and trip mileometers and even pegs for a rear passenger. The pillion passenger must have supple legs, however, for the pegs are mounted on the swinging arm so that they, and hence the passenger's legs, rise and fall with every movement. With someone else aboard, the springs are compressed further and help with

If enduro-riding is your forte then the Honda's superb instruments will be a godsend. Note how the trip can be reset even with a gloved hand.

controlling the bike, for normally unladen there is a massive 33.3 in between the top of the seat and the ground and this only has to be equated with the average inside leg measurement of a rider to see that in most cases there will be a small problem. Luckily, the bike is light enough to be angled and rested on one's leg at standstill without any problems of it falling, but it is a little awkward to pull away, as first you have to push it firmly upright again.

The underside of the XL500S is very clear and smooth with a neat undertray, but this means that only a sidestand is fitted and, in this case, it is far too long. It will only support the bike if the steering is turned to the left and this creates the problem of not being able to use the steering lock, which engages with the wheel turned to the right . . . !

All in all, apart from its minor faults, the Honda XL500S is an excellent dual-role machine and scores over its rivals in more than any other way by its docile and forgiving road manners. Although the headlight is weak, and the steering needs to be turned consciously for corners, the bike is very much at home on the tarmac, and it is quite possible that many people will buy it just as a road bike with no thought about travelling on the rough with it. Yamaha found that with their XT500 and decided to market a roadster version, the SR, and even with exotic multi-cylindered machines, like the CBX and Gold Wing, it must be on the cards that very soon Honda will bring out their own pukka roadster 500cc single.

Engine: transversely mounted, single-cylinder four-stroke of 497cc with four valves per cylinder operated by a single overhead camshaft. One 32 mm carburettor. Maximum power 34 bhp at 6,250 rpm. Kick start.

Transmission: wet multi-plate clutch and five-speed gearbox. Chain final drive.

Frame and suspension: single downtube cradle with telescopic front fork and rear swinging arm with coil-spring/damper units.

Brakes: drum front and rear.

Performance: top speed 91 mph, acceleration over a standing start ¼ mile 15.2 sec. Fuel consumption 52 mpg.

SUZUKI RG500

It was back in 1964 that Suzuki built a square-four, two-stroke racer with disc valves, and they hoped that it would beat its 250cc competitor, Honda. However, in spite of having a respectable 54 bhp to play with, minor problems kept it away from the results and the project was finally dropped. It was to be another ten years before that same basic design saw the light of day again, this time in Makoto Hase's RG500. For two years, the company built racers for their own team riders, until 1976, when they built their first production batch, available to anyone who had the necessary capital. In only a little time, the bikes were snapped up and, although a little down on power from the model that the likes of Sheene was racing, they certainly took a stranglehold of the World Championship 500cc class and put an end to the domination of the four-stroke machine in the guise of MV-Agusta.

Since that time, the RG500 has gone through steady development and minor redesign to remain, in 1979, a very quick machine indeed. Even though a straight-four, two-stroke Yamaha has won the Championship for the last two years, there are few people who believe that the unusual Suzuki doesn't have the edge in power.

The main change in the RG's engine has been the stepping of the cylinders so that the two forward ones are lower than the rears. This lowers the centre of gravity, puts a little more weight on the front wheel and, Suzuki say, saves a little weight. The works' engines have used a 'square' 54×54 mm engine size since 1976, finding that those dimensions provide a little more torque at low speeds than the previous 56×50.5 mm dimensions. The capacity with the square layout is 494.75cc, which is just a little less than the 497.6cc of the oversquare engine. Each piston has its own crankshaft with a power take-off in the centre and each crank has two bearings, a larger one being used in the middle. The con-rods are located between two flywheels and the rod itself is held firmly by small ends which positively locate them sideways. On the works' machines, the running gear is housed in a magnesium block with titanium bolts, which are utilised wherever possible.

There are several reasons why a square-four layout is used, not least being the much better ground clearance than an across-the-frame four when cornering hard. Also, being only two cylinders wide, the bike can be that much slimmer and thus

Tucked away in there is the famous square-four engine which powers the RG500.

offer a smaller frontal area to the airstream. The main advantage of a compact four, however, is the valve design, for a two-stroke engine works much better with disc valves, a layout which is impossible on a four-in-line design. At the end of each crankshaft, there is a gear which drives a shaped disc in a sandwich with an inlet hole strategically placed. Four variable-choke 34 mm Mikuni carburettors are used and they drink a 20:1 mix. As in all high performance two-stroke engines, water-cooling is used and this allows the engine to work more efficiently at higher temperatures and also helps the aerodynamics a little as there is no need to channel air all around the power unit.

The four gears from the crankshafts drive one single gear on a power take-off shaft which then transmits the power to a sintered bronze multi-plate clutch, which is beside the rider's right foot and which is air-cooled. From there, power is taken to the back wheel through a six-speed constant-mesh gear box. The gear change is usually on the left-hand side but, for most British riders, it is transferred to the right. Running with an 8.4:1 compression ratio, the RG500 engine produces a phenomenal 120 bhp at 11,000 rpm with a few more revs, if no more power, available after that. In fact, it is possible to rev safely to 11,500 rpm, but the power drop-off from there is quite marked. Surprisingly, the power delivery of the engine is quite smooth, although there is a kick when the engine reaches 8,000 rpm. At 6,000 rpm, however, there is but 30 bhp and so obviously the performance of the bike is going to be dramatic with another 90 bhp coming on in just another 5,000 rpm. The torque curve of the engine is quite flat, too, with a peak figure of just over 50 lb ft being developed at around 10,000 rpm.

The exhaust system has a great deal to do with the performance characteristics of a two-stroke and the Suzuki engineers seem to have done a great job with their system, which even includes the mandatory silencing which knocks some 20 dba from the bike's piercing wail. Four separate pipes are used, with the front cylinders exhausting just in front of the rear-wheel spindle and the rear cylinders blowing into tubing running under the seat and straight out of the rear.

The power unit rests in a broad Duplex frame, which, as one would expect, is very rigid indeed. Front suspension is by air forks which run at anything from 14 to 21 psi, depending on condition. Normal dampers are used at the front and an anti-dive set-up is incorporated. At the rear, the Suzuki appears to be of conventional design without a monoshock, but the bike features elaborate Kayaba dampers which are a resplendent gold colour. A massive square-section swinging arm is used and the

The bike which, up until 1980, every privateer needed for a good chance at the 500cc World Championship, the Suzuki RG500.

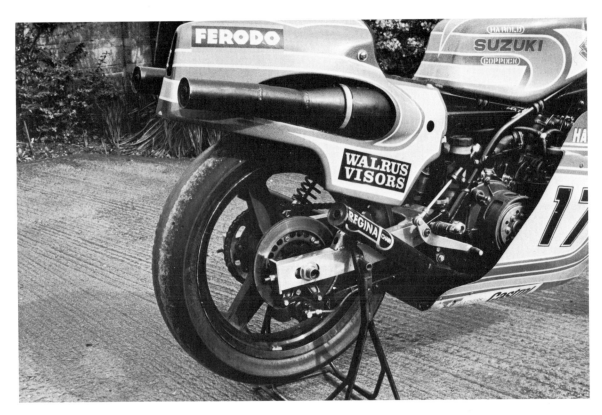

Another example of stout suspension work. Note that this private RG doesn't have Kayaba gold units at the rear: it probably doesn't have the works' bikes' power either.

damper take-off points are well forward of the spindle location.

The special dampers use gas, oil and air for their absorption and there are no mechanical springs at all in the set-up. Braking is by triple disc brakes which are hydraulically operated. The front units are of stainless steel and 300 mm in diameter and are of the self-aligning type; twin piston calipers are used. The rear unit, strangely, is cast-iron and of 230 mm diameter and features air-cooling by slots through the middle running outwards to the edge. The power of the brakes is such that it is quite possible to stand the machine on its front wheel by overzealous use of the progressive lever. The Barry Sheene racer used Campagnolo alloy wheels and ran on Michelin tyres. Several tyre combinations have been used, eg one slick and one treaded tyre either end and then swopped round, but obviously on smooth surfaces more grip is afforded by two treadless tyres. A very rakish body is fitted to the works' RG500s but again the Sheene bike was a little different to the rest. The fairing bears a small resemblance to the 1977 OW31 Yamahas and has a neat tapered underside which ends in a wind-cutting point at the front; the rear body is a fairly deep seat unit which extends to the rear and again tapers to a smooth trailing edge. All motorcycles are quite badly off aerodynamically speaking compared to cars, but the fairings on racing machines like the Suzuki help cut the drag by a huge amount. The drag coefficient for the RG500 will probably be around 0.5 Cx which compares with a figure of at least 0.625 for an unfaired multi roadster and anywhere as low as 0.3 for a sleek coupé car. Of course, a rider who tucks in behind the fairing a lot quicker, and who keeps lower than somebody else, will alter the figures a little, but what has to be remembered is that it takes a lot of power to drive such an unaerodynamic mass through the airstream. High-speed performance depends a lot on wind-cheating, therefore, and it is surprising that, since the days of the dustbin fairings, more attention hasn't been paid to such a significant performance factor. Where Barry Sheene's bike differed from its stablemates was in the placing of two little aerofoils on the fairing, just under the upper line of the front wheel. These helped high-speed stability no end.

The fuel tank depends on what sort of event is entered but the standard one takes 6.9 gal with fuel consumption somewhere around 12-15 mpg. Just as fuel consumption differs, so does top speed and performance, as the many gearing variations can alter the bike's character. For tight circuits, it can be geared to give no more than 135 mph with blinding acceleration, while, for a really long track, a top speed of 180 mph can be plotted, although it is rare for the bike to have enough room to reach such velocities on a closed track.

The Suzuki RG500 is quite a docile machine for its type and in no way is it like smaller two-strokes which can be of the 'all the power or none at all' make up. With a healthy and flattish power curve, the racer can be driven gently but a firm twist on the grip is all that is needed to transform it into a ball of fire. Riding any racer hard is difficult and perhaps the RG is not as bad as most, but any machine which can levitate its front wheels at speeds approaching 130 mph just has to be treated with a great deal of respect.

There isn't much fairing to tuck in behind when the bike is punching through the air at around 170 mph.

Engine: transversely mounted, square-four two-stroke of 497cc. Disc valve induction. Four carburettors. Maximum power 120 bhp at 11,000 rpm. Bump start.

Transmission: dry multi-plate clutch and six-speed gearbox. Chain final drive.

Frame and suspension: Duplex cradle with telescopic air front fork and rear swinging arm with gas/oil/air damper units.

Brakes: twin discs front and single disc rear.

Performance: maximum speed approximately 180 mph, depending on gearing. Fuel consumption between 12-15 mpg.

Again the barest of information for the rider, but he doesn't need much to keep his mind occupied at top speed, so a glance to see that the needles are pointing skywards will suffice.

YAMAHA XT500

In many people's minds the mention of a single-cylinder, four-stroke motorcycle conjures up an image of an old-fashioned British thumper — noisy, black, hellish difficult to start and, more than likely, dripping with oil. That is, however, neither a fair nor an accurate image but it is one the single banger is going to be stuck with for some time to come. One bike which quickly makes a mockery of that image is Yamaha's big XT500 trail bike, a machine which combines some old-fashioned ideals with some brand new applications.

The XT500 was, until the recent advent of the Honda XL500, the biggest trail bike available to the public and proved particularly popular in the United States, for which market it was originally created. The big 500cc engine offered the rider plenty of torque with which to combat the off-road trails, while it also allowed him to ride on the streets in reasonable comfort and at relatively high speeds. For those riders man enough to cope with the punchy engine and the weight, the XT500 was a pretty sophisticated compromise.

The power unit of the XT500 is, as already mentioned, a single-cylinder, four-stroke motor. With a bore and stroke of 87×84 mm, it measures 499cc overall and has a compression ratio of 9.0:1. The engine feeds through a 32 mm Mikuni carburettor and lubrication is by means of a dry sump system. The motor is, of course, different from the old British bangers in that the valves are operated by a single overhead camshaft driven by a chain from the crankshaft. To keep the engine as simple as possible, only single inlet and exhaust valves are used. The pressed-together crankshaft, camshaft and transmission shafts ride in ball, roller and needle bearings. Ignition is by means of a flywheel magneto, the heavy flywheel being fitted to the left-hand side of the crankshaft. The engine itself is remarkably small and compact. The height has been kept to a minimum, which makes for greatly increased ground clearance, an important factor in the design of an off-road machine. The engine is also remarkably vibration-free in comparison to the thumpers of yesteryear and this is

Vying with the Suzuki SP400 and the Honda XL500S in the trail stakes is the mighty Yamaha XT500.

A padded brace on the bars should help a little if you are about to overtake your own bike head first!

Once again, see how uncluttered the under-engine area is on an off-roader, vital for keeping the engine in one piece.

also important to the off-road rider as serious vibration is a fatiguing business. Another important asset to the off-road rider is the fact that the bike is so remarkably quiet. The bike is fitted with a twin-phase, dual silencer system which reduces engine noise to a pleasant chuffing sound. With the silencers out, of course, it does sound like a Manx Norton but as there is little to be gained from this operation, save incurring the wrath of the next-door neighbour, most riders leave the exhaust system well alone.

When it was first introduced, the Yamaha's engine produced a power output in the region of

27 bhp at 5,500 rpm but, over the years, the bike has been developed to the stage where it now kicks out 32 bhp at 6,500 rpm. The power output itself, however, is not so important. What is impressive about the XT500 is its torque. The bike has torque by the bucketful, especially at low revs, and it is this which has attracted so many riders to the big thumper. It really does feel as if it could pull up tree stumps on its own and yet it does it in such a refined manner as to make it completely tractable at low speeds in the dirt.

The XT500's greatest virtue is its ability to rumble along in the dirt at slow speeds and then climb any mountain at the turn of a wrist. It has such a thumping great spread of power that hillsides, muddy bogs and sand dunes can be dispensed with in complete contempt.

Although the big hearty engine is the bike's main feature it would be foolish to overlook the bike's other design features. The five-speed gearbox is both robust and a pleasure to use and the ratios have been well chosen to cope with the contrasting demands of both the dirt trail and the road. Final drive, of course, is by chain.

The XT500's frame consists of a single front downtube and a semi-double cradle complete with

Note how more and more trail bikes are coming with tyres suitable for 'scratching' on the road. You decide if they are wise.

tough sump guard underneath the engine. The front suspension is by means of a telescopic fork, while the rear suspension utilises a conventional swinging arm with adjustable gas/oil dampers. As yet the Yamaha designers have not seen fit to give the big XT500 the monoshock system utilised by the company's two-stroke off-road bikes but that may come in time. In some ways this indicates the thinking behind the XT500. It is not a serious off-road bike. It can be used for enduros or even circuit-racing but it was not designed for it. For competition work the rider will have to develop the bike himself. Yamaha's plan was to give the man who wanted a true dual-purpose street/trail bike something he could get his teeth into.

Consequently, handling is not quite what the motocross ace might demand. At slow speeds the bike's performance is adequate but, once the throttle is turned up, the inadequacies begin to appear. At high speeds in the dirt, the front forks appear to be too soft and the steering tends to allow the front wheel to follow ruts and cracks in the ground that the rider may not want to follow. The rear dampers are too hard by contrast and, at speed, the bike tends to hop from bump to bump which, when you are piloting a bike which weighs over 300 lb (323 lb to be exact), tends to create some alarm within the nervous system. However, as has been said before, the XT500 is no racer and cannot be expected to behave like one. For normal off-road Sunday riding the XT500 is perfectly adequate. It is not for the novice, mind you. The bike's surging power and weight will soon have the novice in all kinds of trouble. In addition, the rider should also be a fairly big, strong man. The bike at saddle-height measures 36 in, which makes it a tall machine. Combine this with the overall weight and it can be seen that the XT500 does require a fair amount of wrestling to ensure that it remains on its own two wheels.

On the street, the XT500 proves to be a thoroughly pleasant bike to ride. Its acceleration is brisk but not shattering and the top speed is around the 90 mph mark, totally respectable considering its dual-purpose personality. The handling proves adequate although attempting to lean the bike over, *à la* Kenny Roberts, could cause some problems. The bike is fitted with dual-purpose off-road/street block pattern tyres which are a good compromise providing neither aspect is taken to extremes. It has, in fact, been known for the XT500 to be fitted with good road tyres and used in this form, together with low-line handlebars, for road-racing purposes. Alternatively, knobbly tyres can be fitted and these greatly increase the bike's performance off-road. For the record, the front wheel measures 3.25×21 in while the back tyre's dimensions are 4.0×18 in. The brakes, drums front and rear, are just about adequate for the dirt but constant high-speed braking on the road will result in serious fading.

A major problem with single-cylinder four-strokes in the past has been starting. Many old bangers require huge amounts of work to get them fired up but the XT500 is a revelation in this regard. It is rare indeed if the XT500 refuses to start after only three kicks and the effort involved is minimal. A prod rather than a full-blooded kick is usually adequate.

For the man who enjoys his off-road riding, the XT500 is about as much as he will ever need. For competition-minded enthusiasts a more modified TT500 is available (in the United States at least) but most riders will find the XT500 more bike than they can handle properly anyway. It is a tough,

rugged bike that is at home in the dirt and yet can cope with any problems street-riding can throw up. If only every motorcycle rider could try the XT500 for ten minutes the old 'oily banger' image that surrounds the four-stroke single could be dispelled forever.

Engine: transversely mounted, single-cylinder four-stroke of 499cc with two valves per cylinder operated by a single overhead camshaft. Single 32 mm carburettor. Maximum power 32 bhp at 6,500 rpm. Kick start.

Transmission: wet multi-plate clutch and five-speed gearbox.

Frame and suspension: Duplex cradle with telescopic front fork and rear swinging arm with coil-spring/damper units.

Brakes: drum front and rear.

Performance: maximum speed 89 mph, acceleration over a standing start ¼ mile 14.9 sec. Fuel consumption 60 mpg.

The business end of the XT which, unlike the monoshock two-stroke Yamahas, is of conventional design.

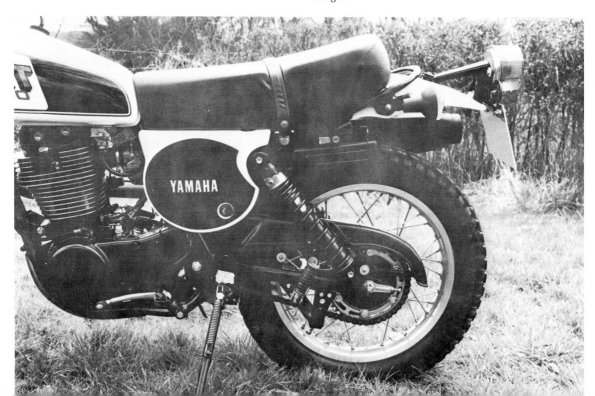

SILK 700S

Although once widely used, motorcycles powered by two-stroke engines are very slowly becoming a rarity these days. Forthcoming legislation controlling exhaust emissions will soon be more restrictive, and the manufacturers once famous for their fiery two-strokes are switching to the cleaner but relatively less exciting four-stroke. Another possible extinction could just as easily occur with the British bike industry, which unfortunately has gradually collapsed since the Oriental invasion during the 1960s. But, despite these changes, there still survives a large capacity motorcycle consisting of both these dying traits. Called the Silk 700S, it is produced by George Silk and a small but dedicated staff at Darley Abbey, in Derbyshire, England.

As a young engineer, Silk took great interest in the virtues of the water-cooled two-stroke engine, particularly that belonging to the Scott marque. This interest led to a partnership between Silk and Maurice Patey, which progressed to the extent that they began specialising in the renovation and tuning of Scotts. When the marque became extinct and engines were no longer available, Silk tried to purchase the production rights from Matt Holder, owner of the Scott name. Unfortunately, this attempt at keeping the Scott alive failed, but Silk had great faith in the engine and overcame the problem by slightly redesigning the power unit. He brought in David Minglow as co-designer and together they sat down and decided to iron out some of the faults associated with the two-stroke engine. These are generally recognised to be poor fuel consumption and a tendency for the exhausts to smoke when under load. The cure came in the form of a patented 'velocity contoured' scavenge system. This differs from the conventional 'loop' scavenge system in that a slightly different piston is used to redirect the gas flow within the cylinder head. When combined with a single Amal Mk 2 carburettor the modifications greatly improved both fuel consumption and low speed torque.

When finally put into production the Silk sported a capacity of 656cc. This has remained the same, but, over the years, the machine has been given a cosmetic face-lift in order to keep up with present trends. Although its traditionally British and rugged looks shine through, improvements have been added in the form of cast alloy wheels, a two-into-one exhaust system and generally updated bodywork. Most obvious is the addition of a tail

An enclosed final-drive chain is just one of the oh-so-sensible items on this svelte British two-stroke roadster.

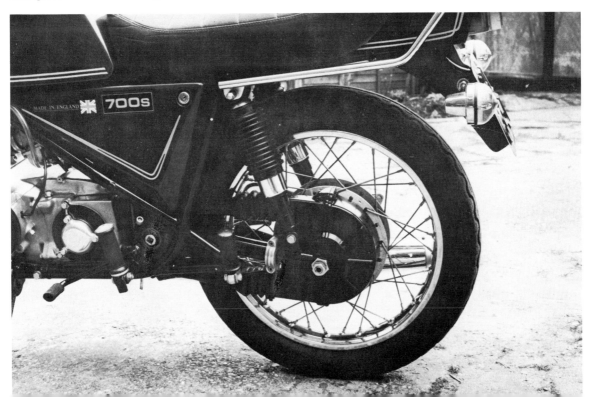

section. This encloses the tail-light assembly and gives the bike a more sporty appearance.

Like its early ancestors, the modern day Silk employs an efficient water-cooling system. Apart from reducing overheating problems, the water-cooling keeps the internal mechanical noises to a minimum. However, on the Silk, the system is rather interesting in that it works on the thermo-syphon principle so no water pump is necessary. The header tank is situated just behind the steering

There is more than a little Scott magic in the Silk engine but that will only endear the 700S to its lucky owner even more.

Unfortunately no longer in production, the Silk will now be a treasured collector's item.

head and this supplies a large radiator that is rubber-mounted to the front downtubes of the frame.

The Silk is started by means of a kickstart situated on the right-hand side. No electric starter is fitted but the bike does not really need one and, in any case, this would destroy the tradition associated with a British machine. Once the footrest has been folded up the kickstart has to be moved back slightly before one is able to kick the engine over. After a few prods, the motor usually comes to life and the resulting two-stroke howl indicates the possibility of an exciting ride ahead.

On the road the rider quickly settles down with no apparent problems and he can soon explore the potential of this unique machine. With high torque at low revs, the Silk will pull like a train, with characteristics more resembling a four-stroke. First gear is rather high and, when moving off, a certain amount of clutch slipping is necessary. Four gears are present and these are located by a 'one up and three down' movement of the left foot. On early models the gear lever was situated on the right-hand side. This has since been moved to the left and it is connected to the gearbox *via* a linkage running across the frame. Surprisingly, gear changing is both smooth and positive and, once top gear is selected, a speed approaching 110 mph can soon be achieved. Initially, the maximum power of 52 bhp at 6,000 rpm could be thought to be rather disappointing; however, when one considers that the Silk weighs a mere 310 lb dry, then its power output is soon forgiven. In fact the power to weight ratio is excellent, a factor which must seem incomprehensible to most manufacturers of today's superbikes.

The most memorable feature of the Silk must surely lie in the handling department. This is where the bike really excels itself. The frame has been constructed by experts, namely Spondon Engineering Ltd, who are famous for their high-class racing frames. This one is no exception. Of the double cradle design, it is both light and extremely rigid. The front gaitered telescopic forks are also provided by Spondon, but, at the rear, Girling Gas Shocks are utilised, along with a conventional swinging arm arrangement. The ride obtained is rather firm but the set-up quickly inspires confidence and bends are taken much faster than one would normally dare. Once a line is chosen, the Silk will stay obediently on course and, if for some reason this has to be altered, then the bike will respond immediately to

A really beefy front end means no fork flexing and superb handling, a feature for which the Silk is renowned.

the rider's commands.

Contributing to these excellent road manners must be the tyres. The ones fitted are the much acclaimed Avon Roadrunners. These give the Silk rider even more confidence, as the bike can be leaned over at quite alarming angles with the tyres refusing to lose their adhesion. Unlike some machines, the bike can also be ridden relatively fast in the rain without fear of losing all when the first bend is encountered.

Just as impressive are the brakes. Made by Lockheed, the front twin discs are extremely powerful, while the rear is equipped with an equally effective drum brake. The good feedback character-

To keep maintenance to a minimum, many parts have been carefully chosen. Electronic ignition is used and the rear drive chain is totally protected by an MZ-type rubber enclosure. Incidentally, when the chain does become slack, adjustment is made by means of a snail cam that is situated near the swinging arm pivot. This method guarantees that the wheel alignment remains true and no checking is necessary.

The Silk is definitely a thoroughbred motorcycle which will obviously appeal to the enthusiast who does not mind paying the price for a quality hand-built machine that is simple, well engineered, and exclusive.

Engine: transversely mounted, twin-cylinder two-stroke of 656cc with piston porting. Single 34 mm carburettor. Maximum power 52 bhp at 6,000 rpm. Kick start.

Transmission: wet multi-plate clutch and four-speed gearbox. Chain final drive.

Frame and suspension: Duplex cradle with telescopic front fork and rear swinging arm with coil-spring/gas damper units.

Brakes: twin discs front and drum rear.

Performance: maximum speed 110 mph, acceleration over a standing start ¼ mile 15.8 sec. Fuel consumption 50 mpg.

A little old-fashioned perhaps, but all the information is there at a glance.

istics aid sure-footed stopping and the units are well on a par with the rest of the machine's high standards.

The riding position is very comfortable, with the rider leaning slightly forward onto wide flat bars. To complement this, the footrests are also well placed and the general layout is perfect for high-speed riding on both country and motorway-type roads. At night, lighting is provided by a 45/55 W quartz-halogen headlamp, which gives all the illumination one is likely to require. The switchgear is basic and functional, while the instrument console houses the usual items, plus an ammeter and two warning lights — high beam and oil.

SEELEY HONDA 750

The fact that a large number of the specialist frame-builders in operation these days have had some experience of racing is no mere coincidence, for it is only under the extreme conditions experienced on the track that the finer points of handling can be explored. However, it is a little strange that, in the case of Colin Seeley, the vast bulk of his racing was done in side-car events, to the point where he was British champion in 1962. During 1966, he became a specialist-solo machine-builder and produced a Matchless G50 powered bike in a chassis that was both elegant and functional; this was the Seeley Condor, a classic road-racer.

After dabbling with a variety of engines, including Suzuki and Yamaha, as well as sundry British units, he began to concentrate his attentions increasingly on the Honda 750 four. With its reputation for durability and its proven performance record, the single overhead camshaft motor was an ideal unit to power his roadster frames. By 1974, the Seeley frame kits and rolling chassis were almost exclusively designed and built to incorporate the big Honda engine, and were then decked out with a variety of American and other accessories, such as Lester wheels, Jardine exhausts, Girling dampers, Lockheed brakes and a variety of big-bore kits. Only items of the highest quality were used and, indeed, quality is one of the hallmarks of the Seeley Honda, from the smooth glassfibre bodywork to beautiful welds that bind the frame tubes together.

The first impression one gets of the Seeley Honda is a visual one. The strikingly compact appearance of the generously wide frame, surmounted by the vast 5.5 gal. tank, together with the little fly-screen and single seat, give the bike a very purposeful air. This is a machine that has been constructed with the rider in mind, a motorcycle to be thrown with abandon into tight bends and to be pitted against all comers on the road.

For many years, motorcyclists the world over have been saying that the ideal machine would be one that combined the reliability and efficiency of a Japanese machine with the handling ability of a

The Seeley Honda is a short wheelbase sportster which means that it is quick to react and an absolute delight when the roads get tight.

The first production Seeley was based on a K2 750 but there is no disguising such a splendid design.

British machine. This is precisely what Colin Seeley set out to achieve with the Seeley Honda.

The Seeley's *raison d'être* is its frame, quite simply one of the best in the world. It is a Duplex cradle manufactured from the incredibly strong Reynolds 531 tubing, and the standard of Seeley's workmanship has to be seen to be believed. All the joints have been hand-matched and the tubing is assembled with bronze welding. As a result of the light-weight materials used in the frame, Seeley has been able to save 25 lb in weight when compared to the stock Honda CB750 frame. Not only is the frame lighter but it is also stronger and less flexible, all characteristics that make for better handling.

The rear suspension on the Seeley Honda is by means of the highly effective American-made S & W multi-rate dampers, while the front suspension employs stock Honda 750 forks. If the Seeley Honda has a fault it lies with these forks in that they are simply not up to the standard of the rest of the bike. At high speed they tend to flex, while fierce braking can sometimes result in a slight juddering. For those riders who demand perfection, however, specialist manufactured forks can be substituted but, of

Standard Honda instruments and switchgear are used, while it seems a shame to tarnish such a tank with petrol.

There is room on the Seeley for one and one only, so they'll just have to believe your stories as to how good it is!

course, that is an expensive business. Bear in mind too, that the complaints levelled at the front forks are only relevant when the bike is travelling at wholly illegal speeds.

The Seeley's other main asset is the marvellous Honda 750 engine. Originally introduced in 1968, it was the Honda CB750 that really established the word 'superbike' in the motorcycling vocabulary. Since that time, many thousands of the four-cylinder units have been manufactured and much development and refinement has taken place. Today, the Honda 750 unit is regarded as one of the most sophisticated and reliable in the world. The basic CB750 engine is a single-overhead-camshaft unit fitted with two valves per cylinder and fed through four 28 mm Keihin carburettors. With a compression ratio of 9.2:1, its 736cc engine punches

An early Seeley, complete with uprated engine and beautiful if impractical white frame.

out 67 bhp at 8,500 rpm. The engine itself is one of the smoothest around and has plenty of torque for smooth take-offs. Indeed, because the mechanical and electrical parts for the Seeley have been supplied by courtesy of Honda, the bike has a remarkable air of reliability and refinement. The latest Honda 750 engine, incidentally, has been developed into a twin-cam unit producing some 77 bhp but, as yet, this engine has not found its way into the Seeley as some modifications would need to be made to the existing frame. The gearbox and transmission unit fitted to the Seeley are also stock

Honda parts. The gearbox has five ratios and the final drive is *via* a chain. The gear change itself is slick and smooth and makes for quick and safe riding.

The combination of stiff frame and flexible engine ensures that the bike is a pleasure to ride. The handling is immaculate and corners can be taken at quite staggering speeds. The Avon tyres, mounted on their attractive Lester alloy rims, also make for good road-holding.

After a hard day's riding, however, the seat begins to feel less than accommodating and the strain of leaning forward onto the narrow handlebars begins to make itself felt in the rider's shoulders and wrists. But, there again, the Seeley was not designed as a long-distance tourer. It is a high-speed roadster, with excellent handling credentials, which is meant to be hurled round corners with great gusto, without any of the encumbrances of passenger or luggage. The amazing frame, together with the multi-rate damping at the rear and the excellent tyres, make the Seeley a very presentable package for the enthusiast rider.

In conclusion, the Seeley Honda provides a very desirable combination of dependable handling characteristics and reliable mechanical function. The lighting, switchgear and instrumentation are all standard Honda items and, as such, are reliable and easily repaired and maintained. Only Honda's front forks can be found wanting but this is a minor criticism. They are perfectly adequate under normal riding conditions. For the rider who really enjoys his riding the Seeley is a must.

Engine: Honda transversely mounted, four-cylinder four-stroke of 736cc with two valves per cylinder operated, *via* rockers, by a single overhead camshaft. Four 28 mm carburettors. Maximum power 67 bhp at 8,500 rpm. Electric start.

Transmission: wet multi-plate clutch and five-speed gearbox. Chain final drive.

Frame and suspension: Duplex cradle with telescopic front fork and coil-spring/rear damper units.

Brakes: twin discs front and single disc rear.

Performance: maximum speed 115 mph, acceleration over a standing start ¼ mile 13.4 sec. Fuel consumption 47 mpg.

TRIUMPH BONNEVILLE

In the twenty years that the Triumph Bonneville has been with us, the world has seen the fall and rise of the Italian motorcycle and a tidal wave of machines from the Orient to suit every taste and need. From being one of the most exciting and revered machines of the late 1950s, the 'Bonnie' has remained largely unchanged and heads towards the '80s in its inimitable style with enthusiastic followers who wish to remain loyal to the 'vintage bike of today'. They will say that, when it comes to handling, there is little that will approach the Triumph, but this is due to the opposition being too blind to catch up with it rather than there being anything magical about traditional British bike design. However, the Bonnie *is* an excellent bike; it is just unfortunate that its story is one of 'more money and lots of development would have made it so much sweeter'.

Nestling in the bike's narrow Duplex frame is the 744cc engine, featuring twin-cylinders and pushrod valves. The motor is of 360° design, so both pistons go up and down together. Deceptively small for its capacity, the engine contributes a great deal (or very little) to the overall weight, which is a mere 400 lb. The engine is undersquare, with bore and stroke measuring 76×82 mm, and runs on a 7.9:1 compression ratio. Power output is just over 50 bhp produced at 6,000 rpm which, although some way off that which one would expect of a multi, is still respectable for a machine of such low weight. For many years, the Bonnevilles were fitted with crude carburettors which had to be manually flooded before starting, but later models feature Amals Mk 2, which save fumbling around either side of the bike before the 'off'. Electronic ignition is also standard on late models but a sad omission is still the electric starter. Although nowhere near as difficult to kick over as a BSA Gold Star, for instance, those used to kicking a two-stroke into life will flinch at the Bonnie. Firstly, one has to make sure that the pillion peg is folded back and those without muscle-bound legs will find putting it on the centre stand and taking one's time will be more effective than a rearward jab at the pedal while seated. When they are running well, one kick is usually all that is needed to get Triumphs into life but the machines are temperamental and may need a lot of coaxing. As neutral has to be engaged before starting, one can imagine the problems that arise for the smaller rider when, for example, stalling in traffic.

It may be a little outdated and a little less than oiltight, but the Bonneville 750 motor is a legend in motorcycling and still pulls like a train.

Once the motor is running, it gives out that characteristic 'British parallel twin' sound, something which reminds one of police bikes and leather-jacketed groups of bike freaks so common in the 1960s. Nice though the sound is, it is accompanied by a fair amount of vibration which gets rather tedious after a while. Also, it makes the rider enforce a rev limit well below the engine's normal red line of 7,000 rpm, as at those engine revolutions the bike feels very fussy indeed. Although again not quite in the same league as

The front end of the Bonneville Special, which can be aimed with the precision that is set aside for only the very best of handlers.

It seems ever more likely that Triumph will soon go under for the last time, which will effectively be the end of the British bike industry.

From this view, the Triumph could be any modern bike; its few detractors can only lay criticism at the engine.

many similar capacity bikes with more cylinders, the Bonnie has nevertheless a surprising turn of speed and the light weight makes it all the more usable. Top speed is around 110 mph, while acceleration over ¼ mile from a standing start takes 13.7 sec. Performance is hindered on the American specification bikes by the large high-rise handlebars and it is hard to lay flat on the tank with one's arms raised so high. The bars are a hindrance even at lower speeds and it is tiresome holding 80 mph or more for anything but the shortest of periods. Somehow on the latest range of Triumphs, the fuel consumption is a little less than one would expect, with 45 mpg being the average one is likely to achieve. Also surprising is the fact that the consumption doesn't alter a great deal either way, whether the bike is ridden gently or hard.

Perched on the dual level saddle, you realise that the suspension is quite firm and indeed it does jar somewhat over rough ground. It is compensated for, however, by the superb feel it gives the bike and one

is always aware of exactly what is being fed into the bike so that it is easy to judge its limits. Even though the American-specification model has bars that are far too high for a lot of high-speed touring, they come into their own when manoeuvring around town, for the machine just begs to be weaved in and out of obstacles, with the upright riding position helping you to sway the bike in and out of traffic. Also, when cornering hard on country roads, they enable a rider to be at just the right angle for judging ground clearance as well as the corners ahead, for the quickest glance down will show just how far away the ground is under the pegs. With a normal 'lean-forward' position, it would be impossible to take such a quick look.

The bike's handling and road-holding are what

you would expect of a Triumph and that is exemplary, with plenty of feel and lots of grip. In fact, the bike feels smaller than it really is and that inspires a great deal of confidence in the rider. It is quite easy to ground the bike on left-handers when the stand digs in quite early, but it is tyre slip which halts progress when cornering to the right. The English-specification Bonneville, with its larger tank and straight bars, is of course the better machine to control when you are really scratching, because the rider adopts a position where weight distribution is better and where it is possible to hang off the machine more readily if the need arises. After a hard run, the tyres feel quite tacky, a sure sign that they are gripping well and that the frame is not hindering their performance too much. Single Lockheed discs are fitted at either end, and they are well up to coping with the performance. They are strong, progressive and actually work well in the wet and are just about as good as you can expect from such a set-up. Sometimes, it was possible to lock the rear brake, but only when the rider was being extremely brutal.

The instruments and switchgear are a little better than previous models, although still someway from being as smooth and attractive as those of Japanese machines. Even though there is a handy cover over the ignition switch, rain will still penetrate the kill switch on the bars, and this caused several 'won't start' problems. In fact, electrics are a common source of problems with Triumphs and it really is unnecessary to have vintage electrics on what otherwise is a fine machine.

The 'Special' series bikes are an addition to the normal range and are distinguished by the black and gold colour scheme and Lester alloy wheels. These are probably the most expensive wheels on the market, and it seems odd that a bike which is already rather expensive compared with its Japanese opposition should have them fitted when another brand would do.

Future development on the bike includes an engine which is rubber-mounted to the frame in much the same way as on the Norton Commando, an eight-valve head for more performance and an electric starter. However, again one would expect these changes and additions to bump up the prices even more and they may take away another portion of the Bonneville's market. What should be done is a lot more development on the reliability side, for three out of the four Bonnies I have tested have gone wrong in one way or another. They can be painful at times when they won't start and they can be annoying when you are togged up with helmet on and they take a dozen or more kicks to fire, but that is forgotten when the engine warms up and you get under way and find an open road. Of course, there is little chance that we shall see a multi-cylinder Triumph for a long while, if ever, and the public is stuck with a twin-cylinder bike whether they love it or not. A bike in the Triumph style that had less vibration, better switchgear, a self-starter, better instruments and a reliable pushrod twin-cylinder engine might not be such a bad bike, though.

Engine: transversely mounted, twin-cylinder four-stroke of 744cc with two valves per cylinder operated, *via* pushrods and rockers, by a single side-mounted camshaft. Two Amal carburettors. Kick start.

Transmission: wet multi-plate clutch and five-speed gearbox. Chain final drive.

Frame and suspension: Duplex cradle with telescopic front fork and rear swinging arm with coil-spring/damper units.

Brakes: single disc front and single disc rear.

Performance: maximum speed 109 mph, acceleration over a standing start ¼ mile 13.7 sec. Fuel consumption 45 mpg.

YAMAHA TZ750

The history of Formula 750, which was originally intended to become the world's premier motorcycle racing class, is one of confusion and missed opportunities. The potential to become the greatest formula was certainly there but somehow it never succeeded. Originally, Formula 750 was created in order to devise a racing class into which the modified 'superbikes' of the early 1970s could be lumped together. In other words it was intended as a production-bike based class, catering for machines like Honda's four-cylinder CB750 and the three-cylinder machines, like the Triumph and BSA triples and the Suzuki GT750 and Kawasaki H2 750 two-strokes.

Then along came the Yamaha TZ750, a full-blooded racing machine built in sufficient numbers to qualify for the FIM's (Fédération Internationale Motocycliste) production limit rule. The TZ750 has dominated the category ever since. The 'superbike' machines, unable to combat the TZ750, simply dropped away and the TZ750 eventually became regarded as the mainstay of the Formula. Kawasaki developed a three-cylinder racer to challenge the TZ750, but it was never really competitive, while Suzuki dabbled with a 650cc version of the RG500 but never built sufficient numbers to get the bike homologated under the FIM rules and so this challenge was confined mainly to British and European 'one-off' events.

Ironically, the success of the TZ750, and the reluctance of its rivals to sustain a serious challenge, may result in the eventual destruction of F750. For 1980, the FIM is withdrawing the category's World Championship status, due to waning interest in the formula, and, with no world titles to aim for, Yamaha may eventually drop the TZ750 model. If this happens the Formula will die a natural death, unless a rival manufacturer steps in with a similar production racer. This, however, seems unlikely. In effect, Yamaha's success could also be its undoing.

The all-conquering Yamaha four-cylinder engine, which has dominated 750cc-class racing worldwide first emerged in 1972. Ironically, it was introduced as the powerplant for a touring roadster,

With no 750 World Championship, the ¾-litre racers, like this TZ750 Yamaha, are a dying breed and their like may never be seen again.

the GL750, at the Tokyo Show in Autumn of that year. The GL750 never went into production, but the water-cooled two-stroke engine reappeared in new racing fettle as the prototype TZ750. Yamaha's first ready-to-race TZ750 made its appearance in May 1973, a limited production run of two hundred motorcycles having been constructed to satisfy AMA (American Motorcyclist Association) homologation requirements. At this time the machine actually displaced 700cc, and two hundred and seventy-one models with this engine capacity were built before October '74, when engine size was increased to a full 750cc.

TZ750s continued to be manufactured in this form until July '76, when a revised model, the TZ750A, was introduced. The TZ750A was incorrectly labelled by the media as the OW31, in fact a factory job number that had somehow been picked up. The label stuck and various sources still describe the works Yamaha machine as an OW31.

Yamaha's current campaigner is known as the TZ750E and, while the factory-supported machine is often described as an OW31, its correct title is in fact the YZR750.

With four cylinders mounted transversely across the frame, the Yamaha TZ series motor is a water-cooled, two-stroke with 'Torque Induction' —

Yamaha's trade name for their reed-valve intake porting. Barrels with seven transfer ports are fitted, and they had a bore of 64 mm and a stroke of 55 mm on the original 694cc unit. The subsequent 750cc motor has a bore and stroke of 66×54 mm.

Early TZs are reported to have developed 90 bhp plus, a very respectable figure at that time, but one eclipsed by the output of the later Yamaha machines, which are endowed with 130 to 140 bhp, depending on who is telling the story.

Steve Baker's YRZ750, which was campaigned in 1977 and '78, is reputed to develop the higher figure, while the production TZ750E models claim the more modest output. There are other differences between the factory-backed YZR and the privateers' TZ750s. For instance, weight is shown as being 309 lb for the works bike as opposed to 326 lb for the production models.

Also, for some reason, the works machines are fitted with Morris cast-alloy wheels where as many privately-entered Yamahas have Campagnolo items. One aspect on which all the competitors seem to

Probably the most powerful engine ever produced for a circuit racer, the 750 Yamaha motor is a veritable gargantuan horsepower producer.

This private TZ750 has two Lockheed discs to haul the 300 lb-plus machine from the enormous velocities of which it is capable.

The screen of the fairing is specially cut out so that the rider can get his crash helmet right up close and offer the sleekest shape to the 160 mph breeze coming his way.

agree is that the powerband of the Yamaha motor tails off at around 11,000 rpm. Where it starts, however, is another matter of differing opinion. Anywhere between 6,000 and 9,000 rpm, according to information, is when the potent 750 begins to accelerate to its 140 bhp peak.

Mikuni carburettors are fitted to the TZs as supplied, and these are mainly retained, though there has been experimentation with the Lectron unit. In usual racing fashion, each cylinder has its own carburettor. Ignition is solid-state equipment supplied by Hitachi, or, in the case of the works machines, by Nippon Denso.

Primary power transmission from crankshaft to gearbox is by straight-cut gears. A dry 7×6-plate clutch controls power input to a six-speed gearbox, and final drive is by Dido or Regina roller chain.

The frame is of Yamaha's own design, a twin-loop cradle, utilising the monoshock or cantilever rear suspension system. A single suspension unit is mounted beneath the fuel-tank, operating in a horizontal plane on the rear wheel *via* a double cantilevered arm.

The first TZ750s used more conventional rear suspension, with vertical coil-spring dampers and rear swing arm, but the monoshock system is now standard equipment on all Yamaha competition machines — on and off-road. Oil-damped telescopic forks are used on the front. Two calipers are mounted on the fork legs to retard double discs, while a single disc and caliper handle rear-wheel braking.

All the brake components, including pads, are manufactured by Yamaha. A 5.1 gal fuel tank fits over the single long suspension strut and beefy top frame tubes, its lower edge following the frame profile. A tiny seat and tail moulding are usual racing practice. Later Yamahas have aerodynamic tail sections partially skirting the rear wheel.

That rear seat-hump is absolutely essential if the rider wants to be there when the bike is accelerating hard!

Exhaust layout on the TZ750 is peculiar in that it routes three pipes to the right-hand side of the bike and one to the left. This very compact arrangement is accommodated by the latest bevelled-belly fairings. Exhaust systems are silenced to meet FIM sound level limits.

Riding the TZ750 is a tricky proposition for all but the most experienced of riders. When it was first introduced, more than a few riders returned to the pits after their first test runs announcing that the bike was too fast to be safe. In time, the majority of riders have come to grips with the TZ's mannerisms but even so the bike is not for the ham-fisted or reckless. Acceleration is nothing less than shattering and great care has to be taken to ensure that the front wheel remains somewhere near the ground on

initial take-off. In addition, injudicious use of the throttle when powering out of corners can result in the rider being thrown off as the back wheel fights for traction, the resultant wheelspin often proving too much for the tyre to cope with. The brakes also take some getting used to. They are immensely powerful and some careful judgement has to take place to ensure that the rider does not either overbrake or leave his braking too late. At the kind of speeds the TZ750 can reach, braking too late can cause the rider to age years in a matter of moments. Little wonder then that even the most skilful of race aces hold the TZ750 in awe.

If the TZ750 is ever phased out of production it will leave behind it a most impressive record. The bike has won two FIM European championships in the hands of Jack Findlay and Victor Palomo, plus three official world titles for Steve Baker, Johnny Cecotto and Patrick Pons. In addition, it has won countless races from America to Australia, from Japan to South Africa. But perhaps the most important of all is the fact that it is the most powerful machine in the history of motorcycling ever to have been offered on sale to the public.

Engine: transversely mounted, four-cylinder two-stroke of 747cc with piston porting and reed valves. Four carburettors. Maximum power 140 bhp at 11,000 rpm. Bump start.

Transmission: dry multi-plate clutch and six-speed gearbox. Chain final drive.

Frame and suspension: Duplex cradle with telescopic front fork and monoshock rear end with gas/oil damper.

Brakes: twin discs front and single disc rear.

Performance: maximum speed 185 mph. Fuel consumption approximately 12-16 mpg.

MOTO GUZZI 850 LE MANS

Who else but the Italians could have built the Moto Guzzi 850 Le Mans? Everything about the machine suggests that it was the work of men who love their work passionately. The Italian nature seems to have an inbred desire for the dramatic, the emotional and the exotic and the Le Mans is a visual symbol of all these characteristics.

The Le Mans has the sleek lines of a racer and a sturdy but light frame that makes for immaculate handling. The fact that the bike's motor only has two cylinders against its Japanese rivals' fours and sixes is of little consequence. The combination of a strong and reliable engine and a frame and suspension set-up that performs so well will, in the hands of a capable rider, prove a match for almost any motorcycle built today.

Part of the reason for the effectiveness of the Le Mans is the policy under which it was built. The men from Moto Guzzi simply were not prepared to compromise the design of their top-of-the-range sportster. The bike was created to be functional rather than fashionable but such is the flair of the Guzzi design team that the end product is beautiful as well. The bike was never meant to be a long distance tourer; it was never meant to carry two people and a tent for hundreds of miles. What it was created for was to be ridden hard over twisty mountain roads by a solo rider looking for the thrills of just such a challenge.

The power unit of the Le Mans is a 90° vee-twin, set across the frame. It has bore and stroke measurements of 83 mm and 78 mm respectively, giving an overall capacity of 844cc. Chrome-plated bores are used, a feature almost unknown on large capacity mass-produced four-strokes. The overhead valves are actuated by pushrods and the engine breathes through two 36 mm Dell'Orto carburettors. The engine is also extremely light, partly because it only has two cylinders and partly because light alloy has been used in the making of the barrels and cylinder head. The engine itself punches out 80 bhp at 7,300 rpm, enough to give the bike a top speed in the region of 125 mph.

Because the vee-twin engine is set so low in the frame, shaft final drive has been utilised. This makes for a smooth ride and eliminates the irritating chain wear problem that so frustrates owners of most high performance machines. The transmission set-up consists of a two-plate dry clutch on the crankshaft *via* spur gears to a five-speed gearbox.

Careful plumbing is needed with the 90° vee-twin's carburettors so that the rider doesn't get a kneeful every time he brakes hard.

The vee-twin engine layout also means that the bike's centre of gravity is low in the frame. This greatly assists good handling which is further aided by the fact that the Guzzi's Duplex cradle frame is immensely strong, giving the bike a superbly steady feeling at high speed. The suspension used on the Le Mans comprises a telescopic front fork with a pivoted rear fork and dampers featuring five-position spring preload adjustment.

The Le Mans is at its best on a long open road. It has a gentle but deceptively quick gait and the superb frame irons out even the most vicious of corners. The riding position is a sort of semi-racer crouch, and the small bikini fairing allows all but the tallest of riders to travel in relatively breeze-free comfort. Because of the smoothness of the engine, and the lazy exhaust note, it tends to feel as though it is going a lot slower than it actually is. It is in fact possible to travel at speeds of up to 115 mph without having to resort to flat-on-the-tank tactics.

The acceleration of the Le Mans is perhaps not as impressive as it might be. It takes a full 14 sec to travel a standing ¼ mile, and this is largely due to the fact that the first gear ratio is fairly high — 11.64:1. In addition, the clutch has a fairly light action and does not seem happy coping with full-blooded take-offs while the shaft drive tends to extend the rear suspension, making wheelspin difficult. Still, what you lose on the straights you

A pillion needs his/her arms round the rider to stay in place. Surely it wouldn't be too difficult for Moto Guzzi to add a grab-rail?

The Moto Guzzi Le Mans Mk II has styling which is a little less brutish than the Mk I, but remains a low and aggressive-looking road burner.

A very tidy 'dashboard' indeed, but many riders prefer the simpler Mk I system.

gain on the roundabouts!

Another unusual characteristic of the Guzzi is that it suffers some torque reaction from the crankshaft when the throttle is blipped or, worse still, when a gear is missed.

For a performance machine, the Le Mans manages to achieve a reasonable degree of fuel consumption economy. Under normal conditions, the Guzzi is good for 40 mpg, dropping to around 35 mpg when given the gun for long periods of time. The fact that only two cylinders need to be fed probably goes a long way to accounting for this fact.

Bringing the 485 lb Le Mans to a halt is also an impressive experience. The bike is fitted with

Guzzi's patented integrated system whereby the footbrake operates the rear disc and one of the two front discs in a 25%/75% ratio. The remaining front disc is operated by the handlebar brake but in most cases it really is not necessary. The footbrake is so well balanced and so effective that footbraking soon becomes the order of the day. In fact, the Guzzi's brakes are about the best in motorcycling. The brakes are also aided by the combination of Metzeler 3.25 × 18 in tyres on the front and 4.10 × 18 in Avons on the rear, a combination which also makes for excellent road-holding.

Apart from its superb handling, the Le Mans's greatest asset is its looks. It is long and sleek and low. The wheelbase measures 59 in while the bike is only 29.5 in at seat height. The fairing gives it a racy look while the 5 gal fuel tank is so attractively shaped that it actually belies its size. It is probably likely that the bike sells as much on looks as it does on performance.

If the Guzzi has a fault, it lies within the electrical system. The switchgear is typically Italian in that it is shoddily designed and executed. This complaint, however, can be levelled at almost every machine that comes out of Italy so at least the Guzzi is not alone. In addition, the speedometer is wildly optimistic. At 30 mph it is already registering 40 mph while an indicated 90 mph is in fact a genuine 75 mph. Little wonder then that Le Mans owners boast so enthusiastically about the performance of their machines.

Electrics aside, however, the Guzzi is a fine machine. It is well made, cleverly designed and sheer enjoyment to ride. The steering is a joy to use and so are the brakes. The engine vibration is but a fraction of that experienced on most big four-stroke twins, while the handling and roadholding is in the pure racer class. The bike is economical to ride yet it is a genuine 100 mph plus runner. It can hold its own with all but the most powerful of machines in top speed and, while the acceleration is not all it could be it, is certainly no slouch. Like most of the Italian thoroughbreds it is fairly expensive to buy but then the bike was designed for enthusiasts by enthusiasts with little thought of penny-pinching in mind. After all, as far as the real motorcyclist is concerned, there can be no price put on the pure enjoyment the Le Mans can offer its rider. That kind of perfection just cannot be measured in terms of money.

The front end of Moto Guzzi's immaculate integral brake set-up.

The rear brake and shaft drive set-up. The whole plot looks very compact and solid and it really is.

Engine: transversely mounted, vee-twin cylinder of 844cc with two valves per cylinder operated, *via* pushrods and rockers, by a single central camshaft. Two 36 mm carburettors. Maximum power 80 bhp at 7,300 rpm. Electric start.

Transmission: twin-plate dry clutch and five-speed gearbox. Shaft final drive.

Frame and suspension: Duplex cradle with telescopic front fork and rear swinging arm with coil-spring/damper units.

Brakes: twin discs front and single disc rear with integral linked system.

Performance: maximum speed 125 mph, acceleration over a standing start ¼ mile 14 sec. Fuel consumption 44 mpg.

MV-AGUSTA 850 MONZA

The MV-Agusta company is to motorcycling what Ferrari is to the world of motorcars — a company which made its name on the Grand Prix circuits of the world and which specialises in the building of road machines which carry all the hallmarks of a World Championship-winning manufacturer.

The Italian company's top-of-the-range model is the 850 Monza, originally known as the 850 Boxer until it was learned that the Boxer name was already owned by another manufacturer. Whatever it is called, however, the Monza may well prove to be the last MV ever. By 1979, the company had ceased its racing activities and, with the wealthy Agusta

The mighty powerhouse of the machine, similar to the units which took the marque to an unprecedented thirty-seven World Championships.

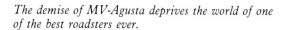

The demise of MV-Agusta deprives the world of one of the best roadsters ever.

family losing interest in motorcycle production — a sideline to the company's racing activities even at the best of times — it is possible that the famous MV name will face from the motorcycling scene.

If MV does disappear, the Monza will make a marvellous epitaph. It is the absolute epitome of what an MV should be — a motorcycle with the grace of a gazelle, the style of a fashion model and the performance of a World Champion racer. If ever a bike had a character and charisma of its own it is the Monza. It is absolutely guaranteed to turn heads wherever it goes.

The 850 Monza model originally started life as the 750 America, which itself was derived from the company's famous four-cylinder 500cc 'fire-engine' Grand Prix racers. The increase in size was an attempt on MV's part to create a machine that could compete on equal performance footing with the multi-cylinder monsters being made by the Japanese, provided the prospective owner was prepared to pay the price. MV's are not exactly cheap and the price — by mid-1979 — of £4,500 made the Monza one of the most expensive machines on the market. The Monza is, therefore, very definitely a rich man's toy.

The power unit of the Monza is a twin overhead camshaft, four-cylinder unit mounted transversely across the frame. It is air-cooled and has a capacity of 837cc. With a four-into-four exhaust system and four 27 mm Dell'Orto carburettors, the elegantly sculptured engine has a claimed output of 90 bhp at 8,500 rpm. It has an electric starter, while ignition is by means of a car-type distributor and twin coils. Pushing the starter produces a rumbling sound from the engine which is followed by the gnashing of camshaft gears, after which the motor bursts into glorious sound. That sound alone has got to be worth the price to the real dyed-in-the-wool motorcycling enthusiast. The carbs make a delicious sucking sound and the complete effect is music to the ears.

The frame of the Monza utilises a Duplex cradle with a single top tube, on top of which sits the massive and attractive 5.2 gal fuel tank and the short suede-covered racing seat. The seat itself can be extended in length to cater for two-up riding but at no time can the experience be described as being comfortable. The Monza is very definitely a one-man motorcycle. The suede seat also causes problems because, although it is very comfortable in

The Monza may not be the prettiest bike ever produced but it would be hard to imagine a bike with more charisma.

the dry, it tends to soak up rainwater and takes days to dry.

Front suspension on the Monza is by means of the highly effective Ceriani front forks which give the bike plenty of road feel and which make fast cornering a joy. The rear suspension is equally effective and comprises a swinging arm and three-way adjustable dampers — usually manufactured by the Italian Marzocchi company, although Koni dampers can also be specified.

Probably the most unusual item on the Monza's specification list is the final drive. Most high-performance motorcycles have chain final drive but

Tommaselli clip-ons, MV embossed instruments and a fire-engine red tank to caress; the stuff of dreams.

MV have chosen to give their Monza shaft final drive. This does have the advantage of eliminating the irritating bugbear of having to tighten or replace chains but it also has a side effect in that it hampers acceleration and adds weight to the machine. Fortunately, however, most Monza owners have probably got beyond the stage of being traffic-light racers so the problem is mostly academic. The gear change itself is excellent, with little of the notchy snatching that is so associated with shaft-drive machinery. The gear ratios themselves are the same as used on the 750 America but, while the America feels overgeared, the extra power of the Monza

manages to make the ratios feel near perfect. The gearbox itself contains five ratios and is operated through a wet multi-plate clutch with a surprisingly light feel to it.

In fact, the Monza is a surprising motorcycle. Perhaps because it is derived from a racing manufacturer, and perhaps because it is Italian, the first-time rider probably expects a rougher ride than he eventually gets. Riding the bike comes as a most pleasant experience. The ride is firm but not hard and the steering is a joy. The bike is very quick and the gear change a pleasure. Most of all, however, the handling is superb. MV-Agusta have won thirty-seven world championship titles in their time and it shows. The bike sits on the road as though it were on rails. It can be flicked through corners at a speed that would startle and confuse almost all of its Japanese rivals and, above all, it feels so safe and sure. The pleasure to be gained from riding a Monza quickly through a series of bends is enormous. It brings a new dimension to motorcycling; every motorcyclist should be allowed to ride a Monza at some stage in his life, if only to rediscover why he took to two wheels in the first place.

In a straight line the Monza is sure and steady. The Monza can be purchased with an optional fairing but it is really only effective if the rider adopts a semi-racing crouch and it also has no protection for the hands. It also hides that marvellous matt-grey engine and, honestly, has not got much going for it, although the cosmetic effect may be worth the £250 it will cost those riders to whom cosmetic effect is important. Mind you, it certainly does give the bike a most racy look.

As far as performance goes the Monza can best be described as adequate. It has an enormous top speed somewhere in the region of 145 mph but it takes a lot of nerve, road and time to get there. It also helps if there are no police around because at that speed the MV is making one mighty spectacular noise. Acceleration is less impressive because of the shaft drive but even so the Monza can trigger the ¼ mile timing lights at around the 12 sec mark.

Two other impressive aspects of Monza motorcycling are braking and fuel consumption. The brakes are excellent, with double discs at the front and a single disc at the rear, and the sure progressive action of the anchors further enhances the excellent feel the Monza provides. Fuel consumption is in the region of 45 mpg, which gives the bike a range of around 200 miles, which isn't unreasonable for a thoroughbred sports machine.

At the time of writing the MV-Agusta company was no longer building machines, although there have been reports that the company may be taken over by everyone from Norton Villiers to Alejandro De Tomaso. So far, however, nothing material has emerged from the welter of rumour and conjecture. Time may well prove the Monza to be the last of a famous line; but, what an exit!

Engine: transversely mounted, four-cylinder four-stroke of 837cc with two valves per cylinder operated by twin overhead camshafts. Four 27 mm carburettors. Maximum power 90 bhp at 8,500 rpm. Electric start.

Transmission: wet multi-plate clutch and five-speed gearbox. Shaft final drive.

Frame and suspension: Duplex cradle with telescopic front fork and rear swinging arm with coil-spring/damper units.

Brakes: twin discs front and single disc rear.

Performance: maximum speed 145 mph, acceleration over a standing start ¼ mile 12.8 sec. Fuel consumption 45 mpg.

NORTON COMMANDO

In this day and age it appears to have become fashionable to belittle the once mighty British motorcycle industry. Whatever the faults of the industry, and whatever the reasons for its downfall, no one can deny that the British industry was responsible for producing some first-class machines and if ever a machine epitomised the best of British it is the Norton Commando 850.

The original Commando model appeared in 1968 and was designed by Dr Stefan Bauer, a talented engineer who had been recruited from Rolls Royce. This model was given the name 'Fastback' because of its all-enveloping rear-end styling and was powered by a 750cc, twin-cylinder engine originally developed for Norton's Atlas models. In time the engine grew to 850cc and the bike was refined until it eventually became recognised as a true superbike in its own right.

When the original Commando was launched the main talking point revolved around the bike's so-called 'Isolastic' frame. In plain English this meant

that the Featherbed-inspired Duplex tube cradle frame featured rubber mounting to reduce the vibration that so plagues large capacity four-stroke vertical twins.

By 1979, the financial problems surrounding the Norton Villiers Triumph group and its various off-shoots meant that production of the Commando had ceased and thus another great British classic was no more. Nevertheless enough Commandos were built to ensure that it is worth a second look, particularly with regard to purchasing a secondhand model.

The power unit of the Commando is a four-stroke, twin-cylinder engine with a bore of 77 mm and a stroke of 89 mm, giving an overall capacity of 828cc. Valve actuation is by the simple but reliable

The testimony on the side of the Commando was proof that certain things could be interpreted in different ways. Electric start didn't mean that it would start by button alone . . .

Like the Bonneville, the Norton is a little outdated, but who could fault the loving care that has been put into the finish of this example?

The Norton Commando has long since passed into history but will never be forgotten by those who rode one or even heard one accelerate at full-bore.

pushrod and rocker system. The compression ratio is rated at a fairly mild 8.5:1 and the engine is fed through two 32 mm Amal carburettors with handlebar-operated cold start slides. In spite of its reasonably mild state of tune the engine can still push out 58 bhp at 5,900 rpm, although the engine gets very breathless if pushed much beyond 6,000 rpm. The engine also features two caged-roller main bearings, plain big ends and dry sump lubrication while ignition is by means of twin coils.

Like most Nortons, the Commando's main asset is its frame. The Norton company's racing heritage has ensured that the Commando frame is among the best in the business. It is light and sturdy with little of the flex so inherent in Japanese designs. Sitting atop the frame is a stylish 5.2 gal fuel tank and a seat that is comfortable enough for most people's tastes.

Front suspension on the Commando is by means of telescopic forks while the rear is catered for by a swinging arm and three-way adjustable Girling dampers. The suspension, however, tends to be a little stiff, with the result that the Commando skitters over smaller bumps making for an unhappy ride on really bad roads.

The Commando's transmission consists of a wet multi-plate clutch with spring diaphragm and a four-speed gearbox. Final drive is by chain. The four gear ratios are well spaced but the vibration set up at high revs makes the rider feel as though a fifth gear might come in useful.

Although earlier models of the Commando used kickstart only, the later model featured an electric starter motor. This was done mainly for the benefit of the American market and the sales brochures because, in practice, the starter motor seemed barely able to turn the big cylinders and a number of owners chose to start their machines on the kickstart anyway.

The original Commando models were supplied with drum brakes both front and rear but, as time progressed, a 10.5 in hydraulically operated disc was fitted to the front and rear. The brakes themselves were excellent as were the tyres, Dunlop K81 4.10 × 19 in, fitted both front and rear.

Once on the road the Commando quickly displays its best characteristics, ie handling, road-holding and steering. The bike's race-bred frame enables the machine to be swung through bends safely and surely. The steering is steady and sure, even at high speeds, while the road-holding, in spite

Even without the name on the tank, the bike would be unmistakably Commando.

of the occasionally bouncy suspension, is first-class. Riders who have been brought up on Japanese multis will, however, immediately notice the vibration. In spite of the bike's rubber-mounted engine, the vibration is still there. It is not unbearable, however, except perhaps at very slow speeds. The quicker the Commando goes, the less the vibration, although revving the engine highly causes the vibration to return.

The undersquare nature of the engine ensures that the Norton has plenty of low-down torque rather than high rev power. This makes for fairly dramatic acceleration and, in fact, the Commando whistles through the ¼ mile in a shade over 14 sec.

Simple and effective: there are certainly no frills about the Norton's instrumentation.

Top speed is also quite impressive — for a bike that is nevertheless 10 bhp down on the average Japanese 750. Speed and acceleration, however, are not really the Commando's forte. Its real strength lies in its ability to cover ground quickly and safely. Few Japanese bikes can even approach the Commando when it comes to handling and only a few of the best Italian bikes could be considered to be on a par with the supposedly old-fashioned British banger. Another strong point on the Commando is that of fuel consumption. Under normal riding conditions the Commando can be expected to return around 45 mpg, which means a useful touring range in excess of 200 miles.

There are a number of other good points on the Commando. The electrics are as good as anything the Japanese produce and the 60 W quartz-halogen headlamp has a strong beam and a well cut-off dip. The switchgear is likewise first-class, while the gear change and clutch action are smooth, slick and light. The bike is also immaculately finished with no evidence of the lumpy welding that is so characteristic of products from the Orient. In addition, the bike only weighs 480 lb which means that it can be manhandled around town with few of the problems which beset owners of certain Japanese machines which shall remain nameless for the moment. It also means that the bike can be set up on its centre stand without too much trouble.

There are a few complaints to be made concerning the Commando. Starting can be a messy business because the Amal carbs still need to be tickled before firing up, while the aforementioned starter often seems most reluctant to spin the engine into life. In addition, the bike doesn't seem to care much for being ridden in heavy traffic at slow speeds.

All these complaints pale into insignificance, however, once the Commando is given the gun. It may have some irritating idiosyncracies but the uncannily safe feeling the Commando transmits to its rider as he swings through a bend at 90 mph makes it all worthwhile. What a pity the Commando is no more. It wasn't perfect but it had character and, for many riders, that is a feature that is sadly missing from motorcycling today.

Engine: transversely mounted, twin-cylinder four-stroke of 828cc with two valves per cylinder operated, *via* push-rods and rockers, by a single side camshaft. Two 32 mm carburettors. Maximum power 58 bhp at 5,900 rpm. Electric start.

Transmission: wet multi-plate clutch and four-speed gearbox. Chain final drive.

Frame and suspension: Duplex cradle with telescopic front fork and rear swinging arm with coil-spring/damper units.

Brakes: single disc front and rear.

Performance: maximum speed 110 mph, acceleration over a standing start ¼ mile 14.2 sec. Fuel consumption 45 mpg.

QUASAR

Originally conceived in 1963, the Quasar is the brainchild of Malcolm Newell who, before committing himself to the Quasar project, was content with the task of designing racing cars. His previous job was aided by a vast knowledge of aerodynamics, a subject which was obviously put to good use in the design of this unusual machine.

As a teenager Newell had owned an enormous number of bikes and as a result he had become a skilled and competent motorcyclist. But he remembered the faults of those machines and bore them in mind when designing the Quasar.

In 1969, Newell teamed up with engineer Ken Leaman, and together they worked to produce a motorcycle based on a functional design philosophy. This design concept led to the inclusion of many innovative features being incorporated on the machine, ignoring the contemporary fashion of motorcycle design which most manufacturers seem to follow. They wanted a bike with definite requirements in mind. These included all-weather protection, safety, comfort, high performance and, perhaps most of all, constructed from British components that were designed to last. What finally evolved was the Quasar.

Financial backing came in 1973 from the small precision engineering firm of Wilson and Sons at Bristol, where Leaman had worked as resident engineer. Admittedly, much time was spent convincing the firm that the bike was a viable project, but they obviously saw the potential as funds came forth for the building of five prototypes. Extensive type approval tests then followed and, despite a programme of crashes, the Quasar came through with flying colours. All that remained now was to concentrate on the task of fullscale production and further space at the Wilson plant was allocated to the Quasar team. By late 1977 production was well under way and firm orders were slowly mounting up.

To appreciate the Quasar fully though, it must surely be ridden and not judged on its impressive looks alone. But preparing to ride the Quasar for the

Like several machines in this book, the future of Quasar is a little less than sure. Is it enough for Britain to say that it produced the world's most radical bike . . . but let it die?

first time can present initial problems. The Quasar rider reclines in a hammock-like seat, which is unsettling at first, but its comfort over long distances soon becomes apparent. Climbing into the cockpit, being careful not to bang your head on the roof, one lifts the machine into the upright position. This is when the weight of the Quasar is fully realised, all 730 lbs with a full tank. The next task is to retract the side stand. The bike is equipped with one each side and these are retracted by pushing and twisting one of the control levers situated just in front of the rider's knees. On turning on the ignition and using the self-starter, the motor readily bursts into life. So far all has been relatively easy but moving off from standstill for the first time can be an amusing event for the inevitable onlookers. Take it easy and the bike wobbles precariously across the road. The only solution is to grab a handful of throttle, grit your teeth and release the clutch, while frantically lifting up your feet as the bike starts moving. Once under way the rider soon settles back into the seat contem-plating the next problem ahead — changing gear. The gear-change mechanism is a two-pedal arrangement situated on the left-hand side. Pushing the top pedal changes up, while the lower pedal is for downward shifts. Each pedal has a large amount of travel and gear changes must be performed slowly and with a positive action, although this is soon mastered.

At the heart of the Quasar lies the power unit, a water-cooled, in-line, four-cylinder Reliant car engine, as used in the popular three-wheelers. Chosen for many reasons, this all-alloy, 848cc motor produces 41 bhp at 5,500 rpm and has proven its reliability over the years. This is exactly what Newell wanted in his original specification, an all-British power unit, that is easily serviced with spares readily obtainable. From the engine, the drive is transmitted to the rear wheel by bevel gears,

Reliant power and low centre of gravity seen in this Quasar under construction.

enclosed in a hub designed specifically for the job by Newell and Leamen. Everything else in the drive train is of Reliant origin, including the single dry-plate clutch, which for a motorcycle is unusual in that it is hydraulically operated.

The Quasar's frame bares little resemblance to those widely adopted by the traditional motorcycle manufacturers. It is a space frame constructed from Reynolds 531 tubing and nylon dipped for long life protection. In the event of a head-on collision the front section of the frame is designed to collapse, thus absorbing a proportional amount of the impact energy involved. Also included are crash bars and a roll bar, making the Quasar rider less vulnerable to injury either when involved in an accident or if the machine is dropped.

Rear suspension is in the form of a conventional box section swinging arm with Girling Gas Shocks as dampers. These tended to be too short for the job in hand, as road shocks were unfortunately transmitted straight to the rider on bumpy stretches of road. At the front, Girlings are again used, but this time complementing leading link forks. Apart from the rear suspension, the handling is excellent and the machine becomes a joy to ride on those long twisting country roads where most conventional bikes are left trailing in the Quasar's wake. Ground clearance is also quite acceptable with only the side stands touching when cornering quickly on a rough section of road. No doubt, poor clearance here must be attributed to the inadequate rear damping. Longer springs with stiffer damping would obviously cure this fault, although at present suitable replacements are not available.

In the braking department, the Quasar is well equipped having hydraulically operated discs at the front and a single disc at the rear. Made from cast-iron they performed admirably in all weather conditions and respectable braking distances can easily be obtained.

After analysing the different types of wheel available, Newell and Leaman decided to manufacture their own. This was mainly due to bearing size and an inefficiency of the available wheels in dissipating heat produced by the discs under heavy braking. Designed to be self-cleaning, the wheels are fitted with tubeless Avon Roadrunner tyres made exclusively for the Quasar. These worked well in both wet and dry conditions, giving the rider predictable road-holding and added safety due to

Folly or design genius? Having been left for dead by a Quasar in the rain rounding a bend at 90 mph, the 90 bhp superbike-mounted author was left in no doubt . . .

their tubeless design.

Unquestionably what makes the Quasar stand out in a crowd must be the futuristic looking bodywork. When conditions turn sour the rider has the advantage over every other two-wheeled enthusiast in that he is kept warm and dry. Made from glass fibre, the fairing has been aerodynamically designed, keeping drag to a minimum and giving better stability at high speed. Incorporated in the fairing is a full length windscreen behind which lie two 75 W quartz-halogen lighting units. These give tremendous illumination after dusk and are complemented at the rear by a large tail-light. Situated between the tail-light and the rider's head is a luggage compartment that is large enough to hold

The closeness of the lights causes confusion when following the Quasar, and that is one of the few criticisms which can be levelled at the bike.

two full-face helmets with ease. In the cockpit another interesting feature is the inclusion of warm air blowers. These direct warm air from the engine *via* ducts on to the rider's hands and are perfect for those cold winter nights. For even more luxury a stereo tape deck or radio can also be installed.

Despite some innovative features the Quasar does have its shortcomings. It certainly has a lack of power, as the engine feels strained when its top speed of around 110 mph is attempted. Gear changing could also be improved, but as previously mentioned the handling can't be bettered. Hopefully the bike will be successful as it would be a shame if this British manufacturer should go the same way as his predecessors.

Engine: Reliant longitudinally mounted, four-cylinder four-stroke of 848cc with two valves per cylinder operated, *via* pushrods and rockers, by a single side camshaft. Single 32 mm carburettor. Maximum power 41 bhp at 5,500 rpm. Electric start.

Transmission: dry single-plate clutch and four-speed gearbox. Shaft final drive.

Frame and suspension: all-enclosing tubular chassis with leading-link front fork and rear swinging arm with coil-spring/gas dampers.

Brakes: twin discs front and single disc rear.

Performance: maximum speed 110 mph, acceleration over a standing start ¼ mile 16 sec. Fuel consumption 60 mpg.

BENELLI 900 SEI

When Argentinian Alejandro de Tomaso invited the motorcycle press to his own hotel in Modena, Northern Italy, in 1972, they came away from the meeting astonished, for he had announced his new Benelli bike. Although a mere 750, its capacity was split up into combustion chambers of 56 × 50.6 mm dimensions which, afficcionados of Honda bikes could easily translate into six cylinders, no less. It was obvious at that time that the prototype displayed was a working bike and one could only imagine and gasp at what its performance would be. It was some time before the Sei staggered into production and unfortunately, however it performed, the accent was by then on 1-litre machines with the emphasis on the 900/1000 Kawasakis for the ultimate in street-scorchers. The factory did try twin-camshaft versions of their 750 but found that its power output was little up on the standard single-cam unit which, after all, was just about a carbon copy of the Honda multi design, itself quite an efficient engine. Strangely, soon after its launch, the Belgian distributors of the marque offered a bored-out 900 version of the Sei to whoever had that much money, and it was this path that the Pesaro company was eventually to take, albeit after the horse had bolted in metaphoric terms. Although again there was a prototype 900 displayed some time before, the Honda CBX and Kawasaki Z1300 sixes were both on the market before the Benelli variant could be offered to the public.

It was late 1979 before the first bikes got into the showrooms and the initial reaction was that they could have been a lot quicker than they were. Basically, 80 bhp just wasn't enough power to cause headlines anymore and, however good the bike was, that fact alone would leave the Benelli out of the reckoning when judging bikes to go into the newly instituted 'hyperbike' class.

The 900 carries on the successful Benelli theme of Honda copy engines and that is no secret on either side. When the 750 was launched it shared just about everything except cylinder finning with the Honda fours and so, given the same high standards of construction, it should give the same reliable performance. The bore and stroke of the engine have been stretched to 60 × 53.4 mm to give a capacity of 906cc, although the compression ratio is a little lower at 9.5:1, as opposed to 10:1. Valve sizes, too, have been adjusted to give the engine better breathing and help low-speed torque, but still only three Dell'Orto carburettors are used which, with their necessarily restrictive manifold, makes them a little less efficient than they might be. As in the earlier bike, the single overhead camshaft operates rockers either side so that the combustion chambers can be hemispherical.

The company claims that the 900 has 15 bhp more than the 750, but as they claim just 80 bhp for the later bike, it makes their 71 bhp quote for the 750 seem a little optimistic now, and that would probably account for its not-too-generous performance. The speed range of the 900 engine is a shade smaller than its forerunner, with peak power being generated at 8,500 rpm and the red line at 9,000 rpm, both figures 500 rpm down on the 750. Drive is taken from the centre of the crankshaft by chain and gears to a dry multi-plate clutch, five-speed gearbox and thence to a huge Duplex chain final drive which has to cope with the constant full-bore performance that any self-respecting rider will surely give the bike all of the time. The whole engine unit is moved further up in the frame in the 900 and this gives better ground clearance, as it really was easy to grind the exhausts away on the 750 bike.

De Tomaso owns both Benelli and Moto Guzzi and, although Benelli only produce two-stroke engines for both marques and Guzzi four-strokes for all, there has been little which has been outwardly similar on either machines, something which would give away their family heritage. The 1979 range of Benellis have changed that, however, and now thankfully there are more bikes using the fabulous patented integral braking system which for so long was only seen on the bikes from Mandello del Lario. The 504 was the first Benelli so equipped and the 900 followed with its triple Brembo discs arranged in the Guzzi way. The 'rear' brake pedal distributes its power 75% to one front disc of 300 mm and 25% to the rear 260 mm unit so that the bike should stop under most circumstances by the right-foot pedal alone. In emergencies or 'sports riding', as the factory says, the handlebar lever will work the other front disc, but surely that is really only there to give riders who are not used to such high technology on motorcycles that extra confidence. It is only the hardened Guzzi rider (and maybe now Benelli pilot) who will put his trust solely in the very capable integral system and leave the other brake alone.

The instruments are a little difficult to read behind the fairing.

The Benelli 900 Sei is very wide and looks unwieldy but under way is somehow transformed into a lithe and seemingly lightweight sportster.

Other notable similarities with Moto Guzzis of
yore are the neat little instrument panel with Veglia
dials and warning lights with embossed
'heiroglyphic' markings and the nose spoiler from
the Mk I Le Mans complete with its dayglo orange
centre section. Surprisingly, the little fairing does
not look out of place on the tallish 900, but is
nowhere near as neat and practical as in the position
of its previous employment. The usual cast-alloy
wheels are utilised, while the expensive Pirelli
Phantom tyres which are fitted are, in effect,
legalised racing covers!

Unlike several other Italian manufacturers,
Benelli have styled their bike themselves rather than
going to a famous design studio, but the end result is
not really too pleasing. Based on their 250 four, the
900 thankfully does not share its little sister's lead
with instruments set into the fuel tank but still has
that 'large tank' look with a miniscule saddle tacked
on almost as an afterthought. Once you ride the 900
and experience the padding, or lack of it, you begin
to wonder whether it really was an afterthought.
The tank itself is a dummy, as there is a steel unit
hidden underneath the glass fibre tank/side panel
unit. The pillion passenger has a grab rail either side
but there really is precious little stopping him/her
from sliding forwards into the rider.

The six-cylinder engine springs to life almost
immediately when the starter is depressed and will
idle without choke a few seconds after. What is
apparent to those who have not experienced a six
before is the complete lack of vibration from the
engine and it really is uncanny with the Benelli.
Unfortunately, the 900 doesn't share the 750's six
separate exhaust pipes and has a more restrained
twin three-into-two system and, although quieter
than its raucous stablemate, no longer has that
growling wail when the throttles are opened. The
muted sound of the 900 is pleasant nonetheless but
no longer will it make the rider blip the throttle in
neutral just for his own aural pleasure and the
annoyance of people who don't understand things
like mechanical music.

The bike is ultra-responsive to the throttle and
the way the engine accelerates through its rev range
is another reminder that this is a six. Acceleration is
a lot quicker than the 750 and the bike has enough
low-speed punch really to storm away from standstill with great verve. Weighing only 488 lb, the
bike has an excellent power to weight ratio and

*So that is where all the bikini fairings of the out-of-
production Mk 1 Moto Guzzi Le Mans went . . .*

gets to the ¼ mile post from a standing start in a
shade under 13 sec and gallops on to the red line in
fifth gear, giving a speed of 124 mph. At this speed,
the little fairing deflects a great deal of the wind over
the rider and one would imagine that a slightly
higher gear could be pulled before the engine would
have trouble in making maximum revs in top. As
the 900 needs to be revved less to get the same sort
of performance as the 750, the fuel consumption is
in fact better, with the bike managing over 40 mpg
on most occasions and returning better than 55 mpg
when only a little throttle is used. With a 5 gal tank,
this means a range comfortably over 200 miles,
although that hard saddle will probably rule out

clearance would be happily traded in for the 750's agility when starting to crank over.

The performance of the Benelli 900 Sei is better than the 750 but still some way off from the Japanese opposition, while the handling and road manners shown are something of a retrograde step from what Benelli has offered in the past. Perhaps we have waited so long for the 900 that we expected something really special, but on the whole one can imagine that most enthusiasts would opt for a 750 with an overbored engine if the factory offered it and wait till either the 900 gets into Mk II guise or an even bigger one appears in a few years time.

Engine: transversely mounted, six-cylinder four-stroke of 906cc with two valves per cylinder operated, *via* rockers, by a single overhead camshaft. Three 24 mm carburettors. Maximum power 80 bhp at 8,500 rpm. Electric start.

Transmission: wet multi-plate clutch and five-speed gearbox. Chain final drive.

Frame and suspension: Duplex cradle with telescopic front fork and rear swinging arm with coil-spring/damper units.

Brakes: twin discs front and single disc rear with Moto Guzzi integral linked system.

Performance: maximum speed 124 mph, acceleration over a standing start ¼ mile 12.8 sec. Fuel consumption 41 mpg.

Round the cylinder finning a little, and whip off two cylinders, and you have a Honda 500 look-alike.

many cross-country trips.

The braking system was something of a disappointment and was nowhere near as well set up as when fitted to the Guzzis. With the Le Mans for example, the brakes could be added to correct mistakes, even when the bike was banked into a corner (something that should never be practiced on any bike really) and would respond by simply slowing down. The higher centre of gravity on the Benelli rules out such foolhardy action and, just as on a conventionally braked machine, the bike will be unbalanced. Also, it seems that the higher engine makes the 900 a little more ponderous when peeling off for corners and sometimes a little ground

DUCATI 900SS DESMO

Ducati's 900SS Desmo stands out in the latest crop of motorcycles as the most uncompromising sports machine available. Fitted with standard equipment which would not look out of place on a race track, the big Duke wears just enough ancillary equipment to get past legal requirements and the dictates of practical necessity.

It is firmly sprung, has a sparsely padded seat, is fitted with clip-on handlebars, set-back footrests and a cockpit fairing. Air-filtration for its intake system is negligible, it has to be kick-started, and the sound level it generates from its nearly straight-through pipes is high. Despite this rather Spartan arrangement, the machine is recognised as a formidable performer in both straight line and cornering departments.

The motive power for the big Ducati is supplied by an air-cooled 90° vee-twin, four-stroke engine of 864cc displacement. Cylinders are arranged one behind the other, so that one is almost horizontal and one almost vertical. Valve gear is peculiar to the Ducati in that it is a desmodromic overhead camshaft system, where valves are opened AND shut mechanically. Valve springs are thus not required, though small hairpin springs are used to seat the valves. There are two valves per cylinder.

Bore to stroke relationship of the new cylinders is decidedly oversquare at 86 × 74.4 mm, with a compression ratio of 9.5:1 demanding the use of premium fuel. The maximum power developed by the Ducati is claimed to be 80 bhp at 7,000 rpm, with maximum torque of 63.5 lb ft at 5,800 rpm. Two huge 40 mm Dell'Orto 'pumper' carburettors meter fuel to the motor. They have neither air filters (apart from wire mesh) nor cold start chokes.

Original right-foot gear selection has been converted to left-hand side actuation to comply with United States federal requirements — a paradox, because the machine fails to comply with several other conditions. Final drive is by 0.625 × 0.375 in roller chain. Overall gear ratios are: 11.74, 8.2, 6.32, 5.25 and 4.66:1.

A tubular Duplex cradle frame is used with the

Ducati produced this Hailwood Replica, based on the 900SS, as their prestige top-of-the-range machine.

40 mm Dell'Orto carburettor, one of a pair, gulps in air to feed the powerful beast.

For high speed stability, a shallow steering head angle (castor) of 59.5° is used, with a long trail of 4.75 in. With a wheelbase of just under 60 in, the Ducati weighs 450 lbs.

Brakes are manufactured by the Italian Brembo works, who supply most of the Italian motorcycles with their equipment. Two perforated cast iron discs flank the front wheel, operated by two double-piston calipers. A single 9 in disc is fitted to the rear wheel. Both systems are hydraulically operated.

Speedline cast magnesium alloy wheels are standard items on the 900SS, the front being a 2.15 × 18 in rim size, while the rear is 2.5 × 18 in. The wheels are shod with M45 Michelins of 3.50 and

Silencer is something of a misnomer for the Conti instrument; it is fitted so as not to silence the savage bark of the big 'Duke'!

engine as a stressed component. The two front downtubes bolt onto the front of the engine and conventional mounting plates secure the back of the powerplant to the frame. This arrangement lends rigidity to the frame, a condition which is ensured at the steering head as well by support from three tubes.

Adequate triangulation at the rear sub-frame provides the inflexibility necessary for swing arm location. Marzocchi suspension components are fitted all round, with telescopic forks using springs and oil damping up front, and coil-spring damper units with five-position spring preload adjustment at the rear.

Marzocchi forks and Brembo discs are used, of course.

Nippon Denso instruments are a small concession to modern electrics afforded by the Bologna company.

4.25 in cross-section dimensions, front and back.

Earlier Ducati 900s had a single seat with a large hump at the rear, but this has been replaced by a dual seat with a much abbreviated tail — looking a little like Yamaha's SR500 seat treatment. The half-fairing remains unchanged — a fixed glass fibre capsule which houses the headlight and instrument panel. The headlight is a CEV quartz-halogen unit of 50/60 W power, and the instruments are by Smiths. A friction damper is fitted through the steering head tube.

The Ducati range has recently been supplemented by the arrival of the so-called 'Hailwood Replica' model. Mechanically identical to the stock 900SS Desmo it is clad in a racing fairing/seat arrangement modelled on the machine Mike Hailwood used to win the 1978 Formula One Isle of Man TT.

The Ducati's notorious noise levels are a result of two Conti megaphone exhausts, and the open carburettor trumpets and gear-driven desmodromic valvegear do their share to enhance the machine's sporty sound. A quick-action throttle twistgrip by Tommaselli completes the list of subcontracted components.

Other standard equipment includes turn signals, trip meter, steering lock, and headlight flasher. Fuel capacity is 3.9 gal and the machine is good for about

50 mpg.

The first impression one gets when astride the 'big Duke' is that it really does feel like a light-weight and indeed that is confirmed when the bike moves off. The pencil-slim machine is very easy to direct even though the steering is a little heavy at slow speeds, and one is soon aware that the 900SS is something very special. Lumpy the engine may feel at low engine speeds, noisy it may sound until you are going quick enough to leave the decibels way behind in your wake and hard the suspension may feel around town and on bumpy roads but when a twisty byway is found the Ducati can be given free rein and left to cross country at seemingly impossible speeds. There are plenty of custom-built roadsters, like the Bimota and the Rickman, which handle excellently, but the Duke has its unique vee-twin engine which gives the whole bike an almost vintage feel in much the same way that a Lotus Seven feels different to a Fiat X1/9 sports car, for example.

There is little doubt that the Ducati 900SS is the closest thing to a racer on the market, and this is perhaps exemplified by the fact that Mike Hailwood on an almost standard machine routed the Japanese opposition in the 1978 Formula One TT. The bike couldn't repeat the dose on the closed tracks of Britain, but the TT course is just like an ordinary country lane that you could find with your Ducati anywhere outside any town anytime. . . .

Engine: longitudinally mounted, vee-twin-cylinder four-stroke of 864cc with two valves per cylinder operated, *via* desmodromic valve gear, by two overhead camshafts. Two 40 mm carburettors. Maximum power 80 bhp at 7,000 rpm. Kick start.

Transmission: wet multi-plate clutch and five-speed gearbox. Chain final drive.

Frame and suspension: twin downtube frame using engine as stressed member with telescopic front fork and rear swinging arm with coil-spring/damper units.

Brakes: twin discs front and single disc rear.

Performance: maximum speed 130 mph, acceleration over a standing start ¼ mile 12.7 sec. Fuel consumption 48 mpg.

SUZUKI BIMOTA SB3

Bimota of the Adriatic resort of Rimini have been very successful with their racing bikes and have scored World Championship titles twice with Walter Villa and his Harley-Davidson-powered machines and once with the Yamaha-propelled bike of Johnny Cecotto. The company offers rolling chassis to take racing engines and invariably they turn out to be a little better designed and a little bit sweeter to ride than the standard machines, which, admittedly, are made in far greater numbers than the few which Bimota produce. Given an identical engine and a rider of similar ability, therefore, it would be safe to assume that the Bimota-equipped pilot will fare a little better than most others. That extra edge makes all the difference in the world of Grand Prix bike racing, but why do people buy road-going Bimotas when there is little competition if any at all on the public roads?

Just as they try to make the ultimate racer, Bimota try to produce the ultimate, and as near to perfect, road bike for the serious rider who has enough money to spend on a bike which, on those rare occasions when the conditions are perfect, will do the least to hinder his pace on a winding road. Around twenty people at the seaside factory lovingly put the bikes together and sell every one of them to buyers who *know* that, however much money they spend, they can get no better than a Bimota.

The KB1 was the first model built and was designed to take the 1,000cc Kawasaki power unit; next along was the SB2 to take the GS750 Suzuki motor and the latest is the SB3, basically an updated SB2 now with the larger GS1000 Suzuki engine as standard. Frame design is essentially similar to the earlier bike, but with some design assistance from Australian racer Jack Findlay, several improvements have been made. Basically, the design of the bike uses the engine as a fully stressed frame member which is enclosed by a chrome-molybdenum steel frame which weighs a trifling 20 lb or so. Viewed from the side, the top tube running from the steering head to the rear suspension is as straight as possible, although of course, from above, it has to bow around the wide cylinder head of the Suzuki engine. That is probably the only hint of compromise in the chassis which in all other respects is an engineer's delight. The rear suspension is the most uncommon feature of the bike because it utilises a car-type De Carbon spring/damper unit placed vertically behind the

The Bimota chassis waiting for its engine looks little more than a sculpture in iron.

transmission and some way back from the swinging arm pivot and attached directly to the arm itself at the bottom and on an aluminium pivot at the top to the frame. The obvious advantage over a normal monoshock system (as used on the KB1, incidentally) is that the SB3 system is so compact. The swinging arm is just about 2 ft long and looks rather ungainly, but it does in fact pivot at exactly the point of the transmission countershaft so that chain tension does not affect the suspension and the suspension does not alter the torque output of the chain, as is the case on conventional designs. Front fork design is interesting, too, and features a steering head whose angle from the vertical is 5° less steep than the fork angle, reducing trail variation under hard braking and thus creating better stability. The design of the frame has just one other trick up its sleeve — it features aircraft-type conical couplings that can be unbolted quickly and simply in effect to split the bike in two for easy maintenance; there is one coupling either side of the frame just by the top of the cylinder head.

A notable change from the earlier Suzuki-powered bike is the addition of a rear sub-frame which features an attachment point for the seat/tank cover unit, with the rider placed now a little more comfortably further back and a little higher. Brembo cross-drilled cast-iron discs are fitted in the usual two at the front, one at the rear formation and either Campagnolo or Speedline cast-alloy wheels are included in the specification.

The ingenious inverted car-type spring/damper unit and its frame-mounting.

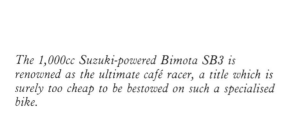

The 1,000cc Suzuki-powered Bimota SB3 is renowned as the ultimate café racer, a title which is surely too cheap to be bestowed on such a specialised bike.

Note the bracing around the steering head and, to the left of the picture, the conical couplings which will later make engine removal simplicity itself.

A sturdy swinging arm, substantial bearings and no doubt impeccable handling. Note how wide the arm is at the pivot so as to stretch round the engine by the power take-off point.

The whole bike is clothed in a very attractive glass fibre body featuring faired-in indicators and rear-lights and a cover for the surprisingly small 3 gal fuel tank. A fairing reminiscent of the KB1 is used and this features a streamlined under-engine section similar to the type first seen on the 1977 Yamaha 750 works' racers.

With a dry weight of just on 450 lb, the 90 bhp of the standard GS1000 is power enough for most road-work and of course the engine is every bit as tractable as its parentage would suggest. Acceleration is almost alarming in its ferocity but the natural crouched position of the rider and the generous rear rider-holding padding disguise the performance most of the time. Traction through the Michelin tyres and finely tuned suspension is impeccable and the bike just lunges forward at an incredible rate with the engine not missing a beat.

Top speed is somewhere over 130 mph if you can find a suitable road, while acceleration over a standing start ¼ mile takes a little over 11.5 sec. You can guarantee fuel consumption of around 35-45 mpg, too, with the weight advantage over a standard bike.

A high-speed run tucked in behind the fairing is not using the Bimota to full advantage, however, and only a trip to the byways will show the machine's advantage over most other two-wheelers. The riding position is a little less ideal than that of the SB2, which was virtually no-compromise road racer in design, but still it puts the pilot in a good position to exploit the chassis' potential to the full. The steering is very precise and the merest thought will turn the bike into a sweep with no fuss at all. Should power be applied or a little braking or even adjustment of one's line be tried, the bike will respond with no fuss and certainly no ill effects. It really does depend on rider nerve just how far one is prepared to go, for the Michelin covers have an outstanding amount of grip and there is nothing at all anywhere near the ground to scrape and give the rider an early warning of the limits of cornering reserves. No, this is a bike for a rider who knows exactly where the limits are and who needs no telltale graunches or weaves to do the job for him. Of course, one has to beware of riding in the wet or on rough surfaces when the tyres can let go, but with such steering response and so much better steering lock than on the SB2, an experienced rider should be able to sort things out.

With 4.5 in of travel at the front and 5.5 in of travel at the rear, the Bimota gives quite an acceptable ride and helps make long journeys less of a chore. That will be made up for though by constant refuelling of the tank, which can empty rather quickly when using all of the speed of which the bike is capable.

Many 'café racers', as machines of this type are sometimes labelled, are very poorly finished when it comes to controls and bodywork, but the Bimota is very much an exception. The instruments and switchgear are straight from the Suzuki, while the fairing and body are constructed of superb quality glass fibre with no crazing or faults. Indeed, it is hard to find fault on the Bimota SB3 anywhere, unless of course you are going to crib at the price, which is approximately £2,000 for a rolling chassis, or £4,000 for a complete ready-to-ride road-burner. It is an awful lot of money for a bike, but it is an awful lot of bike for the money.

Engine: Suzuki transversely mounted, four-cylinder four-stroke of 997cc with two valves per cylinder operated by twin overhead camshafts. Four 28 mm carburettors. Maximum power 90 bhp at 8,000 rpm. Electric start.

Transmission: wet multi-plate clutch and five-speed gearbox. Chain final drive.

Frame and suspension: full backbone frame using engine as stressed member with telescopic front forks and swinging arm rear suspension with single inboard coil-spring/damper unit.

Brakes: twin discs front and single disc rear.

Performance: maximum speed 134 mph, acceleration over a standing start ¼ mile 11.5 sec. Fuel consumption 40 mpg.

Many café racers are let down by their cheap and nasty bodywork, but the Bimota boasts nothing but the best in legendary Italian styling.

BMW R100RS

It is not often in motorcycling that a manufacturer starts a whole new trend, be it technical or aesthetical, but this did happen when BMW introduced their R100RS. As ever, the bike was powered by the venerable flat-twin engine, had shaft drive and was nicely made. What set it apart was that it came with a large fairing as standard. This was not just an ordinary fairing, one that looked out of place and whose aerodynamics were debatable, but one which was scientifically designed and integrated with the bike's overall style. It transformed the bike and led the way for a series of imitation designs appearing in the accessory market and prompted other manufacturers to realise that a fairing could be pleasing to the eye, protective and enhance certain aspects of a machine's performance.

Although the BMW company later built just about the ultimate touring fairing for use on their RT model, the brief for the RS was for bodywork that would aid sports riding, and so the whole would have to be sufficiently low to give that impression. After the initial designs were made, a team from BMW travelled to Turin and set up base at the Pininfarina styling house, home of one of the most famous car design companies. Using that establishment's large wind-tunnel, it was possible to mould a shape that would be ideally suited for the job. It was even possible to add trim spoilers into the design so that a small amount of downforce could be generated at high speeds.

The BMW's engine has grown steadily over the years, although it is hardly likely to get any bigger than its present 980cc. Very oversquare in design, the pushrod flat twin is just about as smooth as you could possibly hope for such a configuration, but nevertheless still feels archaic compared to one of the many multis available. Breathing through two car-type constant-vacuum carburettors, the engine produces a healthy 70 bhp at 7,250 rpm, but after a few miles acquaintance you realise that the engine is far happier further down the rev range; for the most comfortable ride, a self-imposed rev limit of around 5,500 rpm is the order of the day. Power is taken to a five-speed gearbox and thence to a shaft drive

The BMW R100RS created a sensation with its amazing, fairing and no other manufacturer has even come near to producing such an efficient yet attractive design.

From here we see the large fuel tank and the superb protection the fairing gives the rider from the elements. Note the impressive heater system for the feet!

running down the left side of the bike and, in spite of much development work, it is the gear change that is one of the most apparent deficiencies of this expensive machine. Compared to a comparable chain drive bike, the BMW's gear change is slow and ponderous. Even when deliberately taking time over cog selection, the transmission will sometimes let you down and baulk.

The frame of the bike is remarkably strong and never gives even the slightest impression of flexing, even at high speeds. This, combined with well developed ultra-long travel suspension, makes the big BMW a very comfortable machine to ride indeed. It soaks up all manner of bumps with no problem at all and makes light work of uneven

terrain. It is the handling at high speed that causes a great deal of consternation, however, and there are two separate and very different factions for and against the machine. There are devout BMW enthusiasts who think that their bikes are second to none, while there are others who think that the machines are easily the most over-rated handlers on two wheels. While there are no obvious deficiencies when it comes to the swings and roundabouts of country roads, the bike does have a few quirks. The long-travel suspension firstly gives the bike a vague feel and does not inspire the confidence obviously that a stiffly sprung 'café racer' would, for example. Also, when riding really hard through 'S' bends you find that it takes more than a moment to coax the bike from banking right to banking left. A conscious pull has to be made to lift the Bee Em out of the corner and this is strange as it doesn't happen when going from left to right. It is probably the gyroscopic precession in the longitudinal crank which affects it in the same way that rotary-engined aircraft were affected in World War 1, when they could turn on a sixpence one way but needed miles to turn the other.

It is only at the very extremes of cornering speed that this occurs, however, and there is no question that normally the RS BMW is a very handy bike to have for cross-country sprints. The early bikes were fitted with a drum brake at the rear, but a standard three-disc set up was later standardised, along with attractive but very-expensive-to-replace alloy wheels.

Although the BMW's fairing is smooth and low, it gives the machine a far larger frontal area than that of a bare bike with a prone rider. Consequently, the top speed suffers more than on similarly powered models where the rider can hug the tank. Top speed is around 115 mph, while acceleration over ¼ mile takes just under 13.5 sec. The supple suspension makes itself felt again when accelerating hard, for the bike squats on its haunches and bursts forward with the front fork travel lifting right to its stop. With a little more brutality, it is possible to get the 463 lb bike's front wheel into the air, but that is hardly 'BMW style' riding.

When at speed, the fairing comes into its own in most respects, but for riders around 5 ft 10 in it has one rather unfortunate shortcoming. As you lean forward to the low set bars your realise that the top of the screen is just under your eye line.

It looks as if the BMW has a heated window over the headlamp, but the lines are merely for styling; the light never steams up anyway, even in the foulest of weather.

An adjustable steering damper, excellent instruments and adequate switchgear all nestle within the protection of the bodywork.

Consequently, wind blows straight into your face until your reach around 50 mph, when it deflects further up and into the top of your helmet. Riding with a visor down is not that easy at lower speeds either, as there is no air flow to keep it from misting, while ducking behind the screen reduces vision drastically and causes backache. BMW obviously can't keep every size of rider happy but many people have this problem with the RS and, of course, it is doubly troublesome in the rain. Reach an open road and, as would be expected, the fairing is a veritable blessing be it wet or dry, for the screen and lower bodywork keep just about all of the rider free from the elements.

The BMW is quite a tall machine and this, along with the restricting fairing and low bars makes it quite difficult to manoeuvre at low speed, either on it or walking it into a space. This probably has something to do with the bike being aimed at the large rider, for originally the machine's standard seat was only ever of any use if you were 6 ft 2 in or over. Of curious banana-shaped design, it was not really useful for pillions, while still only giving rear support to the long-legged of the species. A more comfortable twin-seat is now available as the standard item, along with a combined luggage rack at the rear which is an ideal base for lots of luggage. Should any more items need to be carried, Krauser panniers are an option which, although expensive, are cavernous and easy to lock onto the bike.

Other changes have been made to the RS since it was announced, and these include the fitting of an oil-cooler and a revision of the switchgear. The original units were extremely well made but somewhat confusing to get used to for the indicators, for instance, had 'up' for left and 'down' for right. Sometimes it was only the very loud, and sometimes annoying, bleeper warning system which reminded you they were on. A more normal arrangement has now been adopted although it is not nearly as pleasing to the eye. Instrumentation is first-class with a voltmeter and quartz clock, supplementing the usual speedometer and tachometer.

Just like the handling, the BMW R1000RS as a whole is very much a love-it or hate-it machine and rarely do you find anyone who has ridden one who has any doubts as to what side to take. BMWs sell as many as they build and usually to the older rider who wants to travel great distances with great economy and great comfort. For a rider who has thrashed 10,000 rpm constantly from a rock-hard-suspended multi-cylinder road-racer, the BMW must represent an unpretentious and efficient next step in motorcycling. Soft, supple and relaxed; just the bike for when 'the tra-la days are over . . . .'

Engine: transversely mounted, twin-cylinder four-stroke of 980cc with two valves per cylinder operated, *via* pushrods and rockers, by a single central camshaft. Two 40 mm carburettors. Maximum power 70 bhp at 7,250 rpm. Electric start.

Transmission: dry single-plate clutch and five-speed gearbox. Shaft final drive.

Frame and suspension: Duplex cradle with telescopic front fork and rear swinging arm with coil-spring/damper units.

Brakes: twin discs front and single disc rear.

Performance: maximum speed 115 mph, acceleration over a standing start ¼ mile 13.5 sec. Fuel consumption 45 mpg.

HARLEY-DAVIDSON XLCR-1000

Harley-Davidson's XLCR-1000 is a radical breakaway from the kind of machine the famous American company normally produces. Over the years the name Harley-Davidson has come to represent the archetypal Stateside motorcycle, a big, powerful and comfortable machine on which to discover the freeways of the land — a tourer to end all tourers.

The XLCR is no tourer, however — not unless the rider is a real sucker for punishment. It is a big, black, mean road-burner, a café-racer built more along European lines than its overweight big brother the Electra Glide. It is also the fastest production bike that H-D have ever built, although that is not actually saying much. The top speed of the machine is only in the region of 115 mph, much slower than its multi-cylinder rivals from Italy and Japan.

Speed, however, is not what the XLCR is all about. The bike's main selling point is the image it creates. With the strictly enforced 55 mph speed limit operational throughout America, speed is now of purely academic interest to the average US rider. What he wants is something which will turn all the heads at the local roadhouse parking lot and that is exactly what the XLCR was designed to do.

The XLCR was originally shown as a styling exercise back in 1974 but was not put into production until 1977. The original design was by Harley's Director of Styling, William G. Davidson, brother of John A. Davidson, president of the legendary Milwaukee company that bears his name. William G.'s design used two bikes as its basis. The

The massive engine dwarfs the tiny fuel tank, and there is little excuse for placing the ignition in such an awkward place these days.

front half used the 1,000cc Sportster engine and frame while the rear end was pure XR750 flat-track racer. To this concoction he added a tiny fuel tank (2.5 gal only), a skinny seat and a mini front fairing, all three items chosen on the grounds of fashion rather than function. The overall result, however, is a bike which is most pleasing to the eye in a peculiarly brutal sort of way.

The real focal point of the XLCR is its massive engine. It is a 45° vee-twin unit measuring 997cc and pushing out 61 bhp at 6,200 rpm,. not a great deal by modern day power output standards. All out power, however, is not greatly important to the XLCR because it has torque in great big gobs, 52 lb ft at a lowly 3,800 rpm. The engine is pure vintage in both design and appearance. Indeed, this fact only adds to the macho image of the XLCR. It really is a great big tough lump of a motor and it seems to have a personality and identity all of its own. The cylinders and heads are made from cast-iron. The huge crankshaft mounted flywheels only add to the rough-hewn image of the bike. The overhead valves are pushrod actuated and the motor is fed through a big 38 mm Keihin carburettor placed between the two cylinders.

In stark contrast to the XLCR's he-man appearance is the fact that no kickstart is fitted. Modern day motorcycle-man apparently doesn't mind a rough ride but he no longer cares to spend his energy trying to kick his evil-tempered beast into life so H-D have compromised and fitted an electric self-starter. Once the choke has been actuated, the carbs primed and the starter button punched, the big motor bursts into life with that rough and curiously off-beat vee-twin note that is so beloved of vee-twin enthusiasts.

The engine of the XLCR nestles within a most sturdy-looking Duplex tube cradle frame and the suspension is by means of a Kayaba telescopic front fork and a rear swinging arm with five-way adjustable dampers. The rear suspension, however, is not all it should be and nor is the damping. Consequently the ride is rough and hard, the bike

The Harley-Davidson XLCR Café Racer is very much a one-off for the Milwaukee company and has never received a fraction of the respect usually set aside for the firm's other wares.

bounding along the road almost as though it had no suspension at all. Add to this the fact that the seat is a decidely flimsy affair, plus the brutal engine vibration, and you get a situation in which it becomes almost impossible to ride the bike for any great length of time. There is only so much pain even the most macho of riders can take in a given period of time. But what the hell, as we said before, the bike isn't meant to be ridden any further than the local drugstore.

In spite of its lack of sophistication the XLCR does boast one or two refinements. Apart from the already mentioned starter motor the bike also has a set of direction indicators. Indeed, all the electrical components appear to have been designed to last a lifetime and the huge solid-looking dynamo situated in front of the engine looks as though it is practically unbreakable. Ignition is by means of a coil and the electrical power is supplied by a 12 V battery placed somewhat awkwardly over the clutch-housing.

Riding the XLCR is an unusual experience, particularly if the rider is used to the smoother mass-produced multis from Japan. The controls of the machine are chunky and the accelerator needs a firm hand to keep the bike on the move. The vibration from the engine is immediately noticeable and so is the glorious bark from the bike's oddly shaped exhausts (the two exhaust pipes are of different lengths). The torque is another thing that is immediately noticeable. The clutch is strong and the gear shift is notchy and stiff. A four-speed gearbox is used but the bike's torque is such that the rider tends to keep the bike in top gear for all but traffic light pull-offs. Besides which the

It must be admitted that there really is very little to the XLCR, apart from the engine, although that is enough for most.

combination of clutch and gear lever action do not really make for slick shifting.

Bringing the XLCR to a stop is another unusual experience but not one that you would want to do very often or in any great hurry. This is not because the brakes are bad but rather because they are too good. With twin 10 in discs up front and a single disc at the rear the bike feels overbraked and it is possible to lock the front brakes quite easily at times, an unnerving experience. The bike is fitted with Goodyear Eagle 3.75 × 19 in tyres at the front and 4.25 × 18 in versions at the rear and the tyres offer good road-holding. The wheel rims, incidentally, are attractive cast-alloy and help to give the bike a very racy look.

Apart from the roughish ride there is one other serious criticism to be made of the XLCR. It has no centre stand, which, on a bike that weighs 520 lb, can make for problems on a surface that isn't reasonably level. In addition it makes puncture repair a tedious business.

In spite of its shortcomings, however, the XLCR makes friends almost wherever it goes. The reason is that the XLCR has a definite personality all its own. Unlike the Japanese multis, most of which are almost carbon copies of another, there is no mistaking an XLCR when it arrives. There's that thundering sound for one thing and that muscular visual appearance for a second. There is just no ignoring an XLCR; you'd have to be blind to miss it in a parking lot. And, let's be honest, that counts for an awful lot when it comes to big bikes. Image is still something which counts a lot with potential bike buyers whether they care to admit it or not. Too bad you've got to be superman to ride the thing for more than 150 miles at a time. Mind you, Superman might have liked the big, black XLCR. It is, after all, a real man's motorcycle, a mean mother of a dude. And, of course, when it comes to image, it really can't hurt to be seen on the back of a Harley-Davidson, can it?

Engine: longitudinally mounted, vee-twin-cylinder of 997cc with two valves per cylinder operated, *via* pushrods and rockers, by a single central camshaft. Single 38 mm carburettor. Maximum power 61 bhp at 6,200 rpm. Electric start.

Transmission: dry multi-plate clutch and four-speed gearbox. Chain final drive.

Frame and suspension: Duplex cradle with telescopic front fork and rear swinging arm with coil-spring/damper units.

Brakes: twin discs front and single disc rear.

Performance: maximum speed 115 mph, acceleration over a standing start ¼ mile 13 sec. Fuel consumption 38 mpg.

HONDA GL1000 GOLD WING

When Honda announced in 1974 that they were introducing a new 1,000cc roadster, most enthusiasts automatically assumed that it would be an out-and-out sports machine aimed at toppling Kawasaki's famed Z900 model from its lofty perch. The design staff at Honda, however, are nothing if not devious and when the Gold Wing, as the bike came to be known, was finally unveiled it proved to be nothing like the bike everybody was expecting.

The Gold Wing was a sporty bike certainly but it was no sports bike. It was quick but it was no racer. In fact, Honda's designers had simply decided it was pointless tackling the Z900 market head on and chose instead to develop a new and even more lucrative market, that of the high-speed, long-distance tourer. As time has proved, Honda's decision was a wise one because the Gold Wing rapidly became a touring favourite, particularly with a multitude of American riders.

The Americans took to the Gold Wing like ducks to water. It was everything they wanted in a tourer. For a start it was cheaper than the rival BMW, considered for so long the ultimate tourer. It was remarkably smooth to ride, extremely quiet, reasonably economical and, above all, utterly reliable. It did not go round corners too well but in America, with its straight, wide open roads, that did not matter at all.

The power unit of the Gold Wing is a four-cylinder motor but it is not of the normal Japanese in-line configuration. Instead, the cylinders are horizontally opposed, the idea being to keep the engine's mass as low down in the frame as possible. The cylinders have wet liners and are pressed into the two halves of the crankcase which are split vertically. The cylinder heads are made of light alloy with the valves in an off-set position. Overhead camshafts are utilised and are driven by toothed belts from the front end. The left-hand camshaft has also been designed to drive the ignition contact breaker while the right-hand cam drives the fuel pump. In a breakaway from tradition, Honda also decided to provide the Gold Wing with liquid-

The Honda Gold Wing has never been a great favourite in Europe but received great acclaim in America where its touring abilities made it the best available. The later 1,100cc version is even more capable.

A flat-four, water-cooled powerhouse, as smooth and silky as any other bike motor and powerful enough to move the bulky 'Wing' with amazing rapidity.

Z900-beater because Honda decided to abandon the chain final drive system in favour of shaft drive. Transmission from the crank is by means of a Morse-type chain to a feather-light wet multi-plate clutch and a five-speed gearbox situated beneath the crankshaft. An idler gear transmits the drive to a spring torsion damper and the drive shaft inside the right-hand fork leg to the rear wheel and spiral bevel gears. The gear change itself is first class, the ratios being neatly spaced and easy to select.

Apart from its unusual engine and transmission, the Gold Wing also sports a number of other technical novelties. It has a fuel gauge, a car-type choke situated on the handlebars, an electric starter and its instruments, on the later models, are to be found in a console placed on top of the dummy tank.

An impressive array of instruments sit atop the dummy fuel tank, looking like an afterthought, which indeed they are.

cooling, the temperature being controlled by a thermostat.

Another attempt to keep the bike's weight low down in the frame was made by placing the 4.2 gal fuel tank beneath the rider's seat. This means that the bike's tank is in fact a dummy unit, housing the air filter, the electrics and a tool tray. The fuel itself is fed to the combustion chambers *via* four 32 mm Mikuni constant velocity carburettors. For their Gold Wing, Honda claimed a power output of 80 bhp at 7,500 rpm and a top speed of 130 mph, enough power and speed even for the most demanding of tourers.

The Gold Wing's transmission proved to be another surprise for enthusiasts expecting a

Shaft drive, Comstar wheels and, here, throaty exhausts which make the bike a little more raspish than the earlier versions.

The Honda's frame is of Duplex tube design and incorporates pressed-steel gusseting; the left-hand side bottom rail is removable for easy engine access. Suspension is by means of telescopic forks at the front and five-way adjustable dampers at the rear. Braking is well taken care of by twin, hydraulically-operated 11 in discs at the front and a single 11.5 in disc at the rear. Since the introduction of the Gold Wing, the original wire-spoked wheels have been dropped in favour of the alloy Comstar wheels now favoured by the Honda designers. The tyres are of Dunlop manufacture and measure 3.50 × 19 in at the front and 4.50 × 17 in at the rear.

Weighing 620 lb dry, the Gold Wing is a handful to manoeuvre in tight situations. Once on the move, however, it becomes a much more manageable proposition. The bike is incredibly smooth. This is partly due to the smooth shaft-drive operation and the gear-change mechanism which is quick, clean and tidy. In addition, the Gold Wing's engine must be one of the quietest in production. It hardly makes a whisper, the only sound being the occasional mechanical click from down below.

The acceleration for such a big machine is surprisingly quick. First gear is fairly low and the bike just rockets away from standstill. 100 mph can be reached in 12 sec while a standing ¼ mile takes a fraction over 13 sec. Top speed is around the 125 mph mark but the rider will need a fair amount of space in which to achieve it.

Bearing in mind that the Gold Wing is

essentially a tourer, the handling is acceptable. In a straight line the bike is a pleasure to ride. It is completely stable and there is next to no vibration whatsoever. When it comes to cornering, however, the Honda is not quite so happy. It doesn't care for being thrown round tight bends and the suspension, when forced to negotiate bumpy bends at speed, tends to react angrily. It is relatively easy to scrape the footrests and travelling through tight bends in a hurry can be a noisy, bumpy, nerve-racking business, definitely not to be recommended. Under ordinary riding conditions, however, the Gold Wing's handling is perfectly adequate. The bike was never meant to be hurled through bends at high speed, it was meant to be ridden two-up mile after mile on the world's highways and by-ways. That is where Honda's Gold Wing earns its bread and butter.

The front end has to cope with the awesome task of hauling the mighty machine down from high speed, which it does with the minimum of fuss.

Engine: transversely mounted, flat-four four-stroke of 999cc with two valves per cylinder operated by two overhead camshafts. Four 32 mm carburettors. Maximum power 80 bhp at 7,000 rpm. Electric start.

Transmission: wet multi-plate clutch and five-speed gearbox. Shaft final drive.

Frame and suspension: Duplex cradle with telescopic front fork and rear swinging arm with coil-spring/damper units.

Brakes: twin discs front and single disc rear.

Performance: maximum speed 124 mph, acceleration over a standing start ¼ mile 13.1 sec. Fuel consumption 37 mpg.

HONDA RCB ENDURANCE RACER

Honda's RCB endurance racing machines have become something of a legend in their own time by completely dominating European long-distance events for three years in a row. Developed specially for the famous six-race series, the Coupe d'Endurance Championship, the indomitable Honda RCB is based on the original CB750 four-cylinder engine with which Honda led the world into our current transverse-four bike revolution.

Honda's intention in producing the RCB was to use it as a mobile test bed for various experiments which would then be transferred to Honda's bread-and-butter models. The alloy Comstar wheels, which can be seen today on a large proportion of Honda production machines, first appeared on the RCB, while the recently introduced Honda 900FZ uses the twin-camshaft engine layout utilised on the endurance racers. Indeed, the success of the RCB was twofold. Not only did it prove a highly useful test facility but it also scored such notable victories on the race track that Honda's prestige enjoyed a highly satisfactory shot in the arm.

The RCB Honda appeared first in 1976, at that time displacing 941cc and developing 115 bhp. Later that year, at the French round of the Coupe d'Endurance, the well-known Bol d'Or, a 997cc version of the RCB made its first appearance. The motor had been bored from 68 to 70 mm. Retaining the original stroke dimension of 64.8 mm, the 997cc version produced 118 bhp at 8,800 rpm. A respectable figure for an engine expected to compete for 24 hours non-stop!

It also produced a whacking 72 lb ft of torque at fairly conservative engine speeds for a competition engine — 8,000 rpm. Not content with this sort of output, the RCB managed an increase in power in 1977 when the original four-into-one exhaust system was replaced with a four-into-two-into-one system. This pushed up the power to about 125 bhp.

These figures are significant when one considers the fact that the RCB powerplant was designed to run at maximum power for 48 hours without break-down. In fact, one of the machines entered by Honda-UK managed 110 hours of racing, and half of that again in practice, without serious problems.

Honda's RCB motor has proved so durable that the teams considered a limit of 10,000 rpm to be more realistic than the previous 9,000 rpm red line. And, in 1979, the engine capacity was raised once more, this time to 1,084cc.

Although based on the CB750 motor, the RCB unit features technical refinements of the kind that render its heritage almost unrecognisable. Its double overhead camshafts, for example, create a profile quite unlike that of the single-cammed CB motor. Also, the casings at each end of the crankshaft have been severely abbreviated to improve ground clearance.

Inside the crankcases, we see numerous differences. The casings themselves are sandcast, with thicker cross-sections for greater rigidity and strength. The crankshaft enjoys larger bearing surfaces and has machined webs in place of the usual forgings. It is a one-piece unit running in five plain bearings, with no flywheel. Primary power take-off is by straight-cut spur gears where the CB motor uses chain. Connecting rods are steel forgings, split at the big end and unbushed to accept a 17 mm gudgeon pin.

In 1976, the RCBs used a lighting generator which was mounted at the left of the crankshaft, charging a 5 Ah wet cell. This was moved in the following year to a position behind the cylinder block and driven by the clutch gear to charge dry cells. Transistorised ignition with a double trigger is used to provide sparks for every 180° of crank revolution. In this way one spark is always in a 'dead' cylinder.

A Duplex chain drives the double overhead camshafts from sprockets in the centre of the crank.

That seat doesn't look very comfortable for a 24 hr ride, but then what seat would be on a bike for that amount of time? Note the 'British' pedal set-up.

Instead of running around sprockets on the actual
camshafts, the chain turns a sprocket and idler gear
on a spindle set into the cylinder head. This in turn
drives gears on each of the two right-hand camshaft
segments. The camshafts are in two pieces, keyed
together by Oldham couplings and each half runs in
three plain bearings. This system is unlike most
contemporary DOHC designs as the idler gear
interface results in the camshafts spinning
backwards in the head.

Cylinderheads are Honda's famous 'pentroof'
configuration, with four valves for each chamber.
The valve seats and spark plug threads are in iron,
and are not inserts, as one would expect, but one-
piece crowns cast integrally in the alloy cylinder
head. A tiny 10 mm spark plug is centrally located
between the generous valves. Inlet valves are 28 mm
in diameter, while the exhaust valves measure 24
mm.

A bank of four 32 mm racing Keihin carburettors
are mounted behind the cylinder head, and they are
of the constant vacuum type. Twistgrip action
operates butterflies in the intake tract, allowing
throttle slides to rise to the demand of manifold
vacuum. This system alleviates any jerkiness in
throttle operation which may arise as riders become
fatigued, as well as reducing twistgrip effort — a
feature to be appreciated after 12 hours in the
saddle!

The engines are mostly hand-made and, in the
interests of durability, are comprised of normal
aluminium alloy castings. The only parts which
have been cast in lighter, more exotic alloys are the
covers for ignition, sump, oil pump, clutch, gear
selector, generator, and camshafts. Because of all
this beefy engineering, the RCB motor is actually
heavier than its progenitor, weighing in at 187 lb.

Power is transmitted from the crankshaft, *via* an
idler gear mounted on a spindle bolted to the
crankcase bottom, to a thin clutch gear which
incorporates a shock absorber comprising six rubber
bushes. The clutch has eight light alloy friction
plates and is controlled by a three-ball ramp release
mechanism which acts on the four clutch springs *via*
a thrust bearing on the magnesium spring housing.

*The big Hondas have swept all before them in
endurance racing where they have proved very fast
and very reliable.*

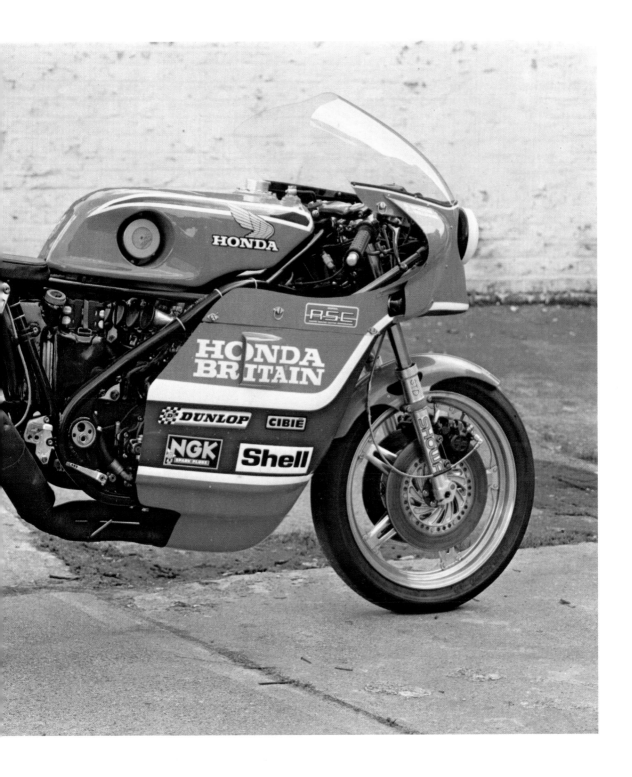

Five ratios are available from the gearbox, which is very similar to the original CB750 unit. To shorten the engine/transmission package, the power input shaft lies above the output shaft. Similarly, to keep the unit narrow, a separate chain sprocket shaft is used, driven off a sixth gear mounted on the inboard side of the output shaft.

Gear selection is by a drum mounted in front of the output shaft controlling three selector forks. The drum is supported at the left by a ball-bearing and at its right side by needle rollers. Two radial roller bearings take care of thrust forces to which the drum is subjected. Engine and gearbox share lubricating oil, of which there is a prodigious 12 pt. It's a dry sump system, hence the large quantity of oil, designed to keep the temperature below 110°C by continual circulation. A trochoid, or eccentric rotor pump with four lobes running in a five-pointed star housing is driven off the kickstart gear on the clutch.

Honda's impressive endurance motor is mounted in a special double-cradle frame developed for the RCB. Telescopic forks with 4.7 in of travel are used at the front with a rake of 27° and trail of 3.45 in. It has been pointed out that this arrangement allows the steering axis to intercept the leading edge of the tyre's contact patch almost exactly.

Gas-damped coil-spring struts suspend the rear wheel, which is a ComStar pattern with 3.5×18 in dimensions. This configuration allows a rear tyre of around 6 in width to be fitted. The front wheel is a more modest 2.5×18 in Comstar item. Three Lockheed disc brakes (two front, one rear) with Ferodo brake pads provide the stopping power.

Weight distribution over the RCB's 58 in wheelbase has been found to be almost exactly 50/50, sharing the machine's mass of 441 lb fairly between the two wheels. With a full 5.5 gal of fuel aboard, the Honda RCB weighs 425 lb.

Because the RCB machines are run directly by official Honda importers, and because they are still currently in action, no examples of the model have ever fallen into private hands. In addition, no journalist has ever been allowed to road test the machines. Consequently, reports on the machine's handling capabilities are confined to off-the-cuff remarks made by those riders chosen to pilot the machines in combat. Most of the riders confirm that the RCB's handling is far superior to that of its road-going stablemates. This is due mainly to the machine's light weight and strong frame. Even so,

the handling is still not perfect, mainly because of the vast power that is transmitted through the frame causing it to flex, albeit slightly. Handling, of course, is not wholly a priority with the RCB because of the nature of long-distance racing. Engine reliability is the prime factor. Nevertheless, the RCB's performance on the race track is quite adequate. The brakes are superb and, with a top speed of around 180 mph, most riders indicate that as a long-distance racing machine the RCB is as good a compromise as has ever been produced. In addition, the care that goes into building each machine ensures that reliability is a big plus factor in the RCB's favour. Indeed, the RCB must go

The intake under the twin Cibie headlamps is to gulp in air for the oil-cooler tucked up inside the fairing.

*Note the wide-mouthed exhaust system and the
mandatory kickstart for endurance-racing rules.*

*The quick-fill system used so that the minimum
amount of time is taken on stops in long races. With
the sort of margins the works' bikes have won by, it
hardly seems worth the trouble!*

down in history as the most successful endurance
racing machine ever produced.

Engine: transversely mounted, four-cylinder four-stroke
of 997cc with four valves per cylinder operated by twin
overhead camshafts. Four 32 mm carburettors. Maximum power approximately 125 bhp at 9,000 rpm.

Transmission: wet multi-plate clutch and five-speed
gearbox. Chain final drive.

Frame and suspension: Duplex cradle with telescopic
front fork and rear swinging arm with coil-spring/damper
units.

Brakes: twin discs front and single disc rear.

Performance: maximum speed 180 mph. Fuel consumption around 20 mpg, depending on gearing.

KAWASAKI Z1000ST

The late 1970s have seen a trend towards large motorcycles with shaft final drive. BMW, MV, and Honda with their Gold Wing, have been using this layout for several years, but it was Yamaha, with their 750 triple and subsequent XS1100, who committed themselves, with a large production run of bikes, to shaft drive. Then with all the advantages over chain drive apparent to a large section of the bike-riding public, other manufacturers joined in the rush to produce their own 'shafters'. Suzuki produced their GS850 which fitted neatly between

The engine which gave rise to the 'sewing machine' theory levelled by lovers of twin-cylinder bikes!

The Kawasaki 1000 is now a whole range of machines, including the latest which features fuel injection. The shaft-drive version has to be the best bet for the tourer, however.

The rear end of the ST looks very similar to that of the Z1300.

the chain-driven 750 and 1000s, but Kawasaki appeared to be indecisive by offering two versions of their 1000, one of each form of final drive. Were they hedging their bets or were they just feeling out the market finally to put their money behind one or the other? Close inspection, however, revealed that the ST was a very different machine to the conventional 1000 Mk II.

A quick glance at the two bikes would tell you very little and, indeed, they both share the same smooth power unit which has become almost legendary in the world of fast biking. Now finished in attractive matt-black, the four-cylinder engine is still a paragon of docility and power. It was around this unit that the familiar clichés of 'turbine-like smoothness' and 'just like a sewing-machine' were given new life. The across-the-frame unit is slightly oversquare and displaces 1,015cc and, in this form, produces 93 bhp at 8,000 rpm and a whopping 65.7 lb ft of torque. The engine's crankshaft rests in roller bearings, slightly stronger

than those of the older versions, and this layout no doubt helps to give the motor that easy running feel. On the inlet side, there has been a revision to 28 mm carburettors instead of 26 mm ones, while for the outlet there is still the four-into-two exhaust system. As usual for Kawasakis, the engine runs at a low compression ratio, in this case 8.7:1, so that low octane fuel can be used. The emission control system on the bike is very advanced and the company takes great care in making their engines as clean as possible. Drive is *via* a wet multi-plate clutch and five-speed gearbox to the shaft final drive, running on the left-hand side of the bike.

Quite surprisingly, the frame of the ST is different from the Mk II 1000, with many of the

Leading-link front forks are to be found on the ST which give it that extra little bit of suspension movement.

As always, the instrumentation on the Kawasaki is exemplary.

detailed improvements first seen on the Z1R. Basically, they have tried to make the chassis stiffer and so flex less under hard cornering, something the ST's predecessors were notorious for. Gussetting has been added to the downtubes and the frame by the swinging arm pivot, areas which are quite critical for good handling. With leading link forks and larger rear dampers, the ST has a lot more suspension travel than its stablemate and this gives the bike a slightly easier ride. Braking is by triple discs and the company uses their sintered-pad system, which they feel is far superior to a standard asbestos set-up in the wet. The discs on the bike are

drilled, not for keeping them cool or dispersing water, but to get rid of brake dirt and reduce squeal.

The ST is quite a tall bike with a seat height of 32.5 in, but, being fairly narrow, it presents few problems. The riding position is very comfortable, but there is still the problem common to machines with fairly high handlebars — that it presents the rider like a sail to the wind which makes long-distance journeys a bit tiring for the arms. The instruments have been revised from the familiar Kawasaki style on this machine and the speedo-meter and tachometer look a little less dated, the latter instrument incidentally housing the now almost *de rigueur* fuel gauge. Another item that has crept into the specification, which is just as welcome, is the one-key ignition/steering lock control situated in the centre of the instrument console. To lock the bars, the ignition key is turned to the left, pushed down and twisted a little more. It does save fumbling under the bike in the dark, for example, which can really be a nightmare. Against the grain of trend these days is the absence of an automatic indicator system, even though the Z1R and top-of-the-range Z13000 have the 'four seconds plus 50 metres system'. However, sometimes having the indicators doused for you is more of a hindrance than anything and you often find that the manual system (available at the touch of a switch on the other big Kawasakis) is preferred by most riders.

Starting the big Kawasaki is easy (as long as you remember to pull in the clutch lever which over-rides the fail-safe circuit), and the choke can be pushed home virtually straight away. Once under way, you soon realise that the shaft drive gives the bike a completely different feel to its chain-drive sister, for only now do you realise how good the transmission is on the Mk II machine. The ST feels a little more ponderous and extra care has to be taken to synchronise engine and road speed when changing gear. Abrupt changes, especially when going into second or first at low speed, can lock the wheel, but this is a trait of all shaft-drive bikes. You just have to teach yourself to expect it with a Kawasaki. Carrying around 60 lb extra weight over the other model does not really make much difference unless you are riding to the limit and even then the chassis variations hide what differences there may be between the two bikes. Quite definitely, however, a small difference shows up when accelerating, for the lighter machine is quicker, as one would expect. There is not a great deal in it on paper (just about 1 sec difference in their respective 0-100 mph times) but it would be quite a few yards on the road.

Slower than the Mk II it may be, but the ST is still a very quick bike taking just over 12.5 sec to reach the ¼ mile post from a standing start, and then galloping on to a top speed just over 130 mph. While this frantic acceleration is taking place, there is little mechanical fuss, just a loud and efficient-sounding scream as the engine begs to be given full throttle. Full throttle doesn't have to be used for good performance, however, for the bike will pick up speed with great gusto in any gear and 'power graph' or 'torque curve' are not things you think about. Such is the refinement and docility of the engine that it is sometimes possible to travel in fourth or even third gear thinking that the selection has been made for top. Use all of the performance all of the time and the fuel consumption should range somewhere between 35-40 mpg, but a consumption of 50 mpg should be easily possible when touring. The bike's fuel tank could be a little larger without being too obtrusive, although with a capacity of 4.8 gal it still offers a good range.

The early 900s and 1000s, and definitely the high-speed Kawasakis before them, were criticised terribly for their handling, and the company has taken great care in improving matters with their 1979 range. There is still a trace that things are not quite right, even though it shows up only when travelling at such speeds that would be foolhardy on public roads. You have to bear in mind, however, that a bike that handles well on the limit of a track will also handle well if need be in an emergency, when quick avoiding action is necessary, for example. Quite simply, the ST is sensitive to throttle openings either when accelerating out of or decelerating into fast corners. Weaving sets in with the power hard on during exits from corners, but it must be stated that it is quite controllable and not the nightmare you think it will be when it first happens.

All in all, the ST Kawasaki 1000 is a nice bike to live with: it has a fine performance, is economical and gets by when called on in its sporting role.

Engine: transversely mounted, four-cylinder four-stroke of 1,015cc with two valves per cylinder operated by twin overhead camshafts. Four 28 mm carburettors. Maximum power 93 bhp at 8,000 rpm. Electric start.

Transmission: wet multi-plate clutch and five-speed gearbox. Shaft final drive.

Frame and suspension: Duplex cradle with telescopic front fork and rear swinging arm with coil-spring/damper units.

Brakes: twin discs front and single disc rear.

Performance: maximum speed 131 mph, acceleration over a standing start ¼ mile 12.6 sec. Fuel consumption 43 mpg.

LAVERDA JOTA

The Laverda brothers are famous in Italy for their range of farming equipment and uniquely styled caravans as well as their road bikes which have a reputation all of their own. Although now the company builds machines with both Husqvarna and Zündapp power, their reputation has been built on their own four-stroke-engined bikes, the most successful of which have been three-cylinder sports bikes. After producing their triple 1000 in various forms, the company decided to market one bike specifically for the British market, using their endurance racing tuning parts and finished off with some very efficient exhausts fitted in England and only legal in the United Kingdom. So, the Laverda Jota was born. From what started as just a highly tweaked 1000, the bike has now acquired a style of its own unique in the range; this has been largely due to its adaption for production bike racing being so successful that the company decided to build it as a racing-style bike in the first place.

'Jota' is the name of a Spanish dance in triple time and this is very fitting for the three-cylinder Laverda of the same name. Unlike most triples, however, the Jota does not have a simple 120° engine with the crank throws equally spaced on the crankshaft. Instead, the Laverda has a 180° engine of similar configuration to a four-cylinder unit, the difference being that this one is just like a four with one cylinder missing. As can be imagined, the Laverda engine will give a very odd sound and a note like nothing else in motorcycling. The engineers at the factory decided on this layout so that high frequency vibration would not suddenly become apparent at high engine revolutions and this is indeed so. What you are left with on the other hand is an engine that will feel quite lumpy and just like a four with one spark plug cap removed, except that the Laverda definitely doesn't *go* like that. The rest of the engine is quite straightforward, with a chain driving twin overhead camshafts between the right-hand and centre cylinders. Breathing is through three 32 mm Dell'Orto carburettors while a high 10:1 compression ratio is used.

In such a high state of tune, the engine produces a whopping 90 bhp at 7,600 rpm, with a very definite upward surge in the power curve just above 5,000 rpm, when the high-lift camshafts start to get into their stride. The engine, in fact, never feels easy until it gets near its red line of 8,500 rpm and will do its best to die on you should you try opening the

Bullet-proof is a term which comes to mind when contemplating the Jota engine.

throttles too much well down the rev range. If you get the impression that the bike is not easy to ride except when it is running hard, you will be quite right. Everything about the machine is geared to speed and everything about the bike makes town work and slow speed work a definite chore.

Power is taken from the engine *via* a massive Triplex chain to a wet multi-plate clutch and on to a five-speed gearbox which, judging from the size of its casing, could easily be a remnant from the combine-harvester line at the Laverda factory. The standard gearing makes the bike a very long-legged machine, although of course there are several options of ratios available for racing which can transform the bike. A chain final drive is used which, surprisingly, doesn't wear too badly, due to the close relationship with the trailing arm pivot and the final drive sprocket.

The engine sits in a narrow cradle Duplex frame which features a massive single backbone tube and plenty of bracing by the steering head and swinging arm and, in all, is a very sound structure indeed. The latest Jotas use the older 1200 Mirage-type frames which have an altered position for the rear suspension mounting, which is of the semi-lay-down type. Corte & Cosso gas dampers are used at the rear and are supplemented by a Marzocchi front fork. Cast-iron Brembo brakes are fitted, which more than adequately cope with the stopping. Laverda was the first Italian company to realise that home-built switchgear and instruments were not really the way to go in the 1970s and so they adopted Nippon Denso units from Japan, which are a much better proposition, being more reliable, nicer to use and better to look at. Since the first Jotas, there have been several changes, with a racer-like single seat with positioning hump being adopted, along with a smaller tank and rear-set pegs. Also, the Jota frame is now painted in Laverda racing silver, which does little to emphasise the obvious quality of the machine.

Without doubt, there is even less compromise in the Jota than the little that was evident in the first models, and this becomes clear when first you stride over the machine and find the bike has about as much distance between the seat and ground as has a pukka motocross bike. Just over 32.5 in separates the rider from *terra firma* and that doesn't inspire a great deal of confidence for controlling the 480 lb bike. When you lean forward to the low bars, it feels even worse. Admittedly, the bars are easily adjusted into an upright position, but then the pegs and saddle are not really suited for that type of set-up. A button is conveniently placed for firing the bike, but with such a high compression engine, the battery has to be fully charged before it can deal with the strain. If, for example, the bike has been ridden for a few hours with the headlight on, as some people do in the daytime and all people do at night, starting again can be a little precarious. If the engine does not fire, there is nothing to do but bump the machine into life and again here the high

An example of the 1979 Jota, minus drilled discs and bikini fairing.

As usual, the most expensive and best items are used, again courtesy of Marzocchi and Brembo.

Forget the 3CL nameplate and the 6,500 rpm redline, this is a Jota complete with those magnificent adjustable bars.

compression makes itself felt as the engine locks the back wheel as the clutch is fed out.

Once running, the motor will sound quite unhappy at idle as the two outer pistons reach top dead centre while the centre one reaches bottom on its own with no other to balance it up. After a few seconds warming up, the engine will settle and will astound people by running at just over 1,000 rpm, missing a beat every three firings and still asking for more. A firm pull is needed on the clutch lever (which again is adjustable for reach) and a hefty prod is needed on the quirky right-hand side gear pedal. A small handful of throttle is needed and, exerting great control over the powerful clutch, it can be eased out to get the bike away. With such high gearing in standard form, the clutch has to be

slipped for a while till the bike gets into its stride and, as you ease along slowly, every beat seems to get through to the rider as the bike appears to move in a series of lumpy jerks rather than at a constant rate. One has to be fierce with the bike to get the maximum performance and it is best to give the bike a helping kick away from standstill with plenty of clutch-wearing slip to get those slingshot starts. Once shifting hard, however, the bike will carry on from there at a reasonable rate, although still very obviously in what would be the wake of a CBX or XS1100. The gear change will not help the rider at all, as it is hard and not too positive. Once the speed reaches around 85 mph, the bike will be near the red line in only second gear and it is here, as the change to third is made, that the Laverda will start hauling in its multi-cylindered rivals from the Orient. By the time the Jota has reached just over 130 mph, with another gear to go, the lead should have changed hands in our imaginary drag race.

Fuel consumption is quite good for such a bike, and the gearing obviously helps here, too, with over 40 mpg being possible under most conditions. If you make use of the mid-12 sec ¼ mile capability and the 140 mph top speed, this figure will be cut drastically, making short work of the 3.8 gal tankful.

Although not the best there is, the handling and cornering ability of the Jota is in the upper echelons of motorcycling, and it will be a very good rider indeed who can provoke the bike into displaying any bad habits. For such a tall and fairly heavy machine, the bike handles astonishingly with the heavy town steering giving way to a positive confidence-inspiring feel as the speed rises. With such impediments as a side stand not fitted, and a compact power unit, there is little to drag into corners as you bank over, and it really is a matter of road surface and rider's nerves giving out before the bike does. The weight of the bike does impair switching direction quickly at high speed on a very twisty road, and it is here where a 900SS Ducati would win over the Laverda with its lightning responses, for example. Braking is exceptional and easily as good as any other bike in wet or dry, even though the rear wheel can lock easily unless care is taken.

The bike is incredibly uncomfortable on long runs, and that sort of use is better set aside from the larger but softer 1200 triples in the Laverda range. When the Jota first appeared, we in Britain thought that we were privileged to have the quickest Laverda available anywhere in the world, through the UK importers Slater Brothers (who incidentally finish the machine off by fitting the very efficient and very loud exhausts). When the bike started to clean up in production bike racing, it was obvious that, for homologation purposes, any improvements needed for the track would have to be incorporated in the roadster. Rear-set pegs mean more ground clearance, while a seat with a rear hump makes for better rider-positioning on the circuit. Expensive air dampers are also handy for 'scratching' at high speed on the track while a silver frame, although looking a little cheap and nasty, is the same colour as the factory racers and will show up any cracks more easily after the bike takes a tumble. Whatever, the

It isn't really hard to see this roadster as a racer, but who is the grab-rail for?

Jota in its latest form should be more successful in racing than before, and who cares if on the road it looks like a racer without the numbers — and goes like one . . . .

Engine: transversely mounted, three-cylinder four-stroke of 980cc with two valves per cylinder operated by twin overhead camshafts. Three 32 mm carburettors. Maximum power 90 bhp at 7,600 rpm. Electric start.

Transmission: wet multi-plate clutch and five-speed gearbox. Chain final drive.

Frame and suspension: Duplex cradle with telescopic front fork and rear swinging arm with coil-spring/gas damper units.

Brakes: twin discs front and single disc rear.

Performance: maximum speed 140 mph, acceleration over a standing start ¼ mile 12.4 sec. Fuel consumption 36 mpg.

RICKMAN ENDURANCE

It has become a well known fact that many of the multi-cylindered 'superbikes' emanating from Japan do not have the chassis to match up to their performance potential. However, such was their power output that they were bought up in vast numbers by the motorcycling public, who were generally willing to forgive them their shortcomings in handling in exchange for the reliability and consistency of the engines. There were people, of a slightly more discerning nature, who felt that an ideal state of affairs could be reached by mating the Oriental engine to a proven frame, and thus a market developed for an accessory frame that would transform a fast wobbler into a fast handler.

In the early part of 1974, the Rickman company launched a rolling chassis for the Honda 750 four motor. In its original guise as a 'café racer', it had a few shortcomings but it was a marked improvement upon the standard frame when it was being pushed around bends in the road at speed. As the brakes and suspension underwent improvement, the Rickman was further modified to accept the Kawasaki 900/1,000cc four-cylinder motors, which brings us to the Endurance variation of the original café racer concept.

This particular machine utilised the standard Rickman frame and differed from the CR mainly in respect of the glass fibre cosmetics and the final drive ratio. However, this difference is not to be belittled as it not only changes the appearance of the bike but also gives a marginally more comfortable riding position. The Rickman Endurance derives both its title and its appearance from the machines used for long-distance racing at events such as the Bol d'Or, where both the stamina of the riders and the reliability of their machinery is put to an extreme test. With this sort of heritage behind its pedigree, it is to be expected that this bike is most at home travelling at speed on the twists and turns of the country lanes.

The Rickman is sold as a rolling chassis, and all that needs to be added to the mix are a suitable Kawasaki engine and instruments. The bike's frame is a normal Duplex cradle built of Reynolds 531 chrome-molybdenum tubing which is nickel-plated

The Rickman Endurance is underneath the skin the same machine as the company's famous café racer.

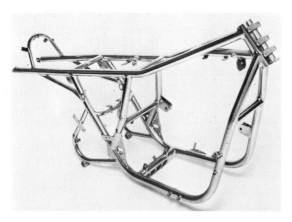

The very heart of every Rickman, the nickel-plated frame made of chrome-molybdenum tubing.

after the construction. Although the finish is quite attractive, with an almost golden tinted chromium look, a few days outside will make the nickel darken and a great deal of care is needed to keep the finished product in pristine condition. That is of little relevance anyway, as the frame does what is intended of it and that is to keep everything rigid when forces are exerted upon it in corners. Earlier Rickmans were fitted with Campagnolo alloy wheels and ultra-efficient cast-iron Brembo disc brakes, but with Kawasaki now supplying their bikes complete with alloy wheels and their own cross-drilled discs with sintered-steel brake pads, these are fitted on to the finished machine, thus saving a fair amount of money. However, Spanish Betor front forks have

For the first time, standard Kawasaki wheels are used, thus saving a lot of money over the previous Campagnolo items.

You can gather from this shot that the rider will be well protected in all weathers.

been used which are far superior to the standard Kawasaki units.

Rickman have designed a very practical fairing indeed with their CRE and it features a neat yet protective front which gives adequate protection for the rider's hands yet doesn't look too ungainly or bulky. Twin headlamps are used and there are also large rear-view mirrors. The CRE has a twin saddle mounted into the bodywork which hangs almost pannier-like over the upper tubes of the frame. It should be pointed out that the fairing has to be removed to perform even the simplest of operations, such as changing plugs and checking points. This little exercise is extraordinarily tedious and is further complicated by the fact that there are six

nylon screws which attach the fairing to the glass fibre tank cover, besides the other eight bolts, plus the indicator mountings, which have to be loosened before the cowling will come away. However, all these mounting points do ensure that the super-structure is immensely secure and doesn't develop any unwanted tendencies towards flexion when being pushed at speed, so what you gain on the roundabouts you lose on the swings.

The excellent twin headlight set-up is mounted on the primary support bracket, which is attached to the steering head, and thus can be easily adjusted when the fairing is removed. The quartz-iodine Cibié lights function independently of each other, with only one burning on low beam and both on high beam. They are sufficiently bright to enable one to cruise around 90 mph at night should you choose to do so.

However nice a bike may be when tearing around the highways and country lanes, there will always come a time when one has to try and negotiate heavy urban traffic and in this sort of congestion the Rickman Endurance really lives up to its name. The limited steering lock imposed by the handlebar/fair-ing arrangement makes weaving around stationary vehicles very difficult indeed and the heavy work that this entails reminds one forcibly that a semi-racing crouch is a less than ideal position when not going anywhere in a hurry and with the motor getting steadily hotter behind the cowling.

The austere black and white colour scheme complements the flowing lines of the fairing and seat unit and an admiring crowd can be virtually guaranteed wherever the bike is parked. However, there is one small drawback to this: it also attracts pillion passengers who beg to go for rides. This turns out be a major error if the trip planned happens to be further than a few miles, since the positioning of the passenger footpegs is conducive to severe cramp and the sloping seat means that the unfortunate passenger slides straight into the rider, which can hamper retardation no end in a tight situation. So despite its attractive appearance the Rickman Endurance is very much a solo affair and the limited accommodation offered for passengers, combined with the ridiculously high rear footrests, only serves to emphasise this fact.

However, one should not dwell too long upon these very minor defects, since this creature must necessarily be viewed as a purpose-built piece of

Extra protection, extra lighting, but the Endurance's lines are nowhere near the classic shape of the famous CR.

steering geometry was well laid out and the bike tracked perfectly at high speed, being light and stable with a very forgiving nature. The Rickman could be made to change direction with the merest shift in body weight and never left the rider feeling flustered out of a corner. The suspension was taut and firm, giving a good feel of the road surface, without bouncing or juddering over uneven ground. the riding position was well tailored for high-speed, long-distance riding and, despite its shortcomings in traffic, it gave one an unbelievable sense of unity with the bike once the speedometer was indicating three-figure speeds.

All in all the most impressive fact about the Rickman Endurance was its immense stability and total rideability once it was on the open road. It steered precisely, handled well and would hold high top gear speeds for hours at a stretch without faltering. The lighting is excellent and the fairing affords a large degree of protection from the elements. It is without doubt a machine for single-minded fast trips with a thoroughbred chassis and an unburstable engine, and well deserving of its title.

Engine: Kawasaki transversely mounted, four-cylinder four-stroke of 1,015cc with two valves per cylinder operated by twin-overhead camshafts. Four 28 mm carburettors. Maximum power 93 bhp at 8,000 rpm. Electric start.

Transmission: wet multi-plate clutch and five-speed gearbox. Chain final drive.

Frame and suspension: Duplex cradle with telescopic front fork and swinging arm with coil-spring/damper units.

Brakes: twin discs front and single disc rear.

Performance: maximum speed 136 mph, acceleration over a standing start ¼ mile 12 sec. Fuel consumption 45 mpg.

transport, and its purpose is to take a rider at high speed from one place to another, under all conditions and at any time of day or night. One could perhaps comment that a larger capacity fuel tank would have been more in keeping with the bike's image, but the Kawasaki motor was suprisingly frugal on the test, returning a steady 45 mpg at consistently high speed, giving the machine a usable range of 150 miles.

The Pirelli Phantom tyres initially appeared to be a little too narrow for a motorcycle as powerful as the Endurance, but they were wonderfully predictable and held the road with immense tenacity, allowing the machine to be banked over to the limit without ever showing signs of breaking away. The

SUZUKI GS1000S

Of all the current crop of superbikes, the Suzuki 1000 series is the most conservative in both design and specification, but that is not to say that it offers the least. In fact, for the smaller rider, the Suzuki offers the most manageable package, for, with a weight just over 500 lb, it is quite easy to handle. The 1000 was a natural development of the earlier 750, and the first variant was the EC/HC which featured rear air dampers.

The GS1000S was first seen in late 1978 and was announced formally in early 1979. Surprisingly on this model, designed to be the top of the Suzuki range, ordinary coil-spring/damper units were fitted at the rear, the company stating that these were better suited for production racing, which is exactly what the bike was built for: an homologation special. Other differences between the 'S' and the ordinary 1000, apart from the obvious cosmetic changes, are slightly larger carburettors, a larger rear wheel and a slight increase in power.

The engine of the 1000 is of the now classic four-cylinder across-the-frame type, air-cooled and driving the rear wheel by chain through a five-speed gear box. Of oversquare dimensions, the 997cc twin-overhead-camshaft engine produces 90 bhp at 8,000 rpm; breathing is through four 28 mm Mikuni carburettors. Again, as is usual with engines of this type, there are no power bands as such, with just a smooth and steady flow right up to the red line.

It is apparent when first getting astride the bike just what a comfortable seat the big Suzuki has and, just when you think that the bike is far too tall, it compresses to hold you snugly with the upmost comfort. Unlike the standard 1000, the S has flat bars, so you lean forward slightly and are not perched up high in the airstream. Further to streamline the machine and rider is a nose fairing, although its effectiveness, apart from upsetting the machine's

Virtual de rigueur now for the superbike, the four-cylinder twin-cam engine.

*A very nice instrument set-up indeed on the Suzuki,
with very neat placing of the choke. Note the steering
lock which is incorporated into the ignition switch.*

*The Suzuki flagship up until the arrival of the
GSX1100, the GS1000S finished in the pre-
sponsorship Suzuki racing colours.*

appearance, is debatable. The screen features a cut-out which is presumably to save the instruments being obscured, while it has what can only be described as a token gesture to a bib spoiler moulded on the underside. As only the upper surface resembles an aerofoil, there is little chance that it will be of any benefit at its minute angle and, even if it did work, it is putting weight on the forks rather than on the main mass of the bike, which would be the most sensible thing to do. In practice, the bike goes through a small period of instability around 105-115 mph and one wonders whether the fairing does upset it.

The example tested had only covered a couple of thousand miles and somehow the bike's engine felt tight. Its performance was well up to expectations, but the power unit did not feel as smooth as many other Japanese multis or, definitely, as the refined engine one comes to expect from Suzuki. At its idling speed of just over 1,000 rpm, engine noise and vibration was quite noticeable and the smaller carburetted GS1000 seemed a much more civilised unit.

Performance was quite spectacular, however, with the standing start ¼ mile taking just a shade under 12 sec and the top speed of 128 mph coming up soon after. What is obvious after a spirited ride is that, even changing gear way before the maximum power of 8,000 rpm the performance is still good enough to leave most other vehicles behind. Even so, fuel consumption remains on the good side of 40 mpg, no matter how hard the bike is used.

Again, after the delights of the HC 1000, the S seems something of a disappointment when it comes to handling. Like all 1000s, the S features the racing-style air front forks which can be adjusted anywhere between 11 and 17 psi, depending on road conditions and the amount of weight carried. On the top of each fork leg is a nut which hides an air valve; simply attach a bicycle hand pump (never use a garage forecourt air-line) and adjust accordingly; high pressure for two up on smooth roads, low pressure for bumpy roads one up, and anywhere in between for whatever you want. What could be a lot easier is not having to adjust each leg individually, as is the case now.

Without the air dampers at the rear, the variations on suspension tuning are not quite so large but, even so, there is still scope to get the ideal ride/handling combination, although obviously

That little fairing which may have something to do with a high-speed stability problem on the bike.

there is still a greater chance that you can be blinded with science and never get what you want. Whatever way it is adjusted with the S, it is difficult to get the same fabulous handling experienced with the standard bike, even though the same settings were tried. The S is still excellent, but the other bike is that much better. Although the larger rear wheel of the S is meant to give more warning of breakaway with its lower profile, somehow the ideal balance is lost.

The Suzuki's frame is remarkably rigid and it is really hard to upset the chassis, even when charging hard in the confines of a test track. The lower than standard bars give the rider plenty of control at high speed and the bike responds well. It was just when powering hard out of corners that the machine felt a little inferior to its stablemate, and then only when trying really hard. Another criticism which comes to mind when using a lot of performance is that the gear change is somewhat slower and less positive than, for example, a Kawasaki's.

On the other hand, braking is excellent in both wet and dry conditions, the triple disc brakes being of a quality that is hard to believe, considering they are just ordinary stainless steel units. They are powerful but never fierce in the dry and give quite extraordinary feel in the wet with no hesitation whatsoever. Because of the bike's agility, you forget that it weighs 524 lb and that makes you think that the brakes, too, are really something special.

As is customary these days, extra instruments have been added underneath the little fairing and, although the quartz clock is quite useful, and the fuel gauge handy, the oil temperature gauge is really unnecessary and only saves a little boredom on long motorway journeys: it is interesting to see by how much the oil temperature falls when it is raining, for example! Styling on the whole is not the Suzuki flagship's long suit and its paintwork of white with a large blue stripe is a little 'boy racerish', even if at one time, before sponsorship came in, they were the company's racing colours. (The same style of finish with a red stripe is also available.) The two large circular mirrors also spoil the machine's lines and, when one considers the tasteful black with pinstripe

machines built by the same company, the S does seem a little garish. It depends on taste really, but what is apparent is the high standard of finish of the bike . . . except for a piece of trim inside the fairing which pulled away while at high speed on the motorway.

On paper, the Suzuki GS1000S may not be the most exciting of current superbikes, and may not be the fastest, the most economical or cheapest, but it offers almost the perfect compromise. That may not be what Suzuki wanted when they built the bike, but that has definitely not detered the buyers, who rate the machine as the most civilised superbike available.

Engine: transversely mounted, four-cylinder four-stroke of 997cc with two valves per cylinder operated by twin overhead camshafts. Four 28 mm carburettors. Maximum power 90 bhp at 8,000 rpm. Electric start.

Transmission: wet multi-plate clutch and five-speed gearbox. Chain final drive.

Frame and suspension: Duplex cradle with telescopic air front fork and rear swinging arm with coil-spring/damper units.

Brakes: twin discs front and single disc rear.

Performance: maximum speed 128 mph, acceleration over a standing start ¼ mile 12 sec. Fuel consumption 40 mpg.

VAN VEEN OCR1000

Henk van Veen was the Dutch importer of the small German Kriedler racing bikes and small roadsters and also dabbled in outboard motors for boats. A wealthy man, he decided back in the early 1970s to produce the ultimate motorcycle and spared nothing in realising his dream. In 1972, he had a prototype on the road and to say that the bike was unconventional would be a serious understatement. Nestling in the bike's Motor Guzzi V7 frame was the engine and gearbox from a Mazda RX2 sports car, and a quick inspection would have confirmed your suspicions that, yes, it was a Wankel engine sitting there. Henk van Kessel put a lot of work into that first tatty looking prototype, not the least being the conversion of the gearbox to suit a motorcycle. There are still arguments about how you classify a Wankel engine with its three separate combustion chambers, and whether you count one chamber, two or three. The Mazda engine, as fitted in the Van Veen, was a twin-rotor design, mounted longitudinally so that the rotors revolved around a shaft at 90° to the line of the axles. The twin-lobe unit featured chambers of 573cc each, so that the capacity was either 1,146cc, 2,292cc or a whopping 3,438cc, depending on your views. For the sanity of mankind, engineers chose the middle computation and so the Van Veen was merely a 2-litre bike with around 130 bhp on tap . . . .

Not long after the arrival of the prototype, Mazda started to wind down their Wankel programme as the rotary engines were very thirsty, noisy and prone to wear out their rotor lobe sealing tips with alarming speed. Only in the late 1970s, with the arrival of the Mazda RX7, is Felix Wankel's design being given a new birth, but that didn't help Van Veen who wanted his own engine. Luckily, around 1974, Citroën were busy building their Wankel-engined GS and, although it never got into production, a small run of cars was constructed for public evaluation. The engines for these cars were manufacturered by the Citroën subsidiary Comotor and here was a chance for Van Veen to get his desired motors.

Unlike the prototype, the production machine's engines are mounted transversely with the rotors

The Van Veen OCR1000 with its Wankel engine looked set for a long stay on the market but vanished before more than a handful were completed.

spinning along the centre line of the bike. Again, a twin-rotor engine is used with 996cc in each chamber giving a 'real' capacity of 1,992cc. Naturally, for such an engine, water-cooling has to be employed, with extra cooling in this case by oil for the few moving parts in the design. The Wankel works on a simple principle similar to a two-stroke engine, so there are no valves or valve gear to worry about. Induction is taken care of by a single 32 mm Solex DDITS carburettor while Bosch Jaeger/Hartig electronic ignition looks after the sparks. Drive is taken from the engine through a dry-twin disc clutch to the four-speed gearbox. Clutch actuation is hydraulic so is very smooth and progressive. After spending a geat deal of money on the engine, Van Veen wasn't going to skimp on the rest of the bike so he commissioned Porsche of Stuttgart to design a suitable gearbox. Only four ratios would be needed as Henk thought that the engine's power and torque would make ratio-swapping a little less important than on a conventional superbike. He was

talking in terms of 100 bhp at 6,000 rpm and an enormous 98.5 lb ft of torque produced at 5,000 rpm. The famous car firm came up with the required item along with a neat shaft drive.

The engine and transmission needed to be seated in a sturdy frame, so Van Veen asked Jaap Voskamp to supply a suitable piece of ironmongery. Jaap was no stranger to sound designs as he worked with Kriedler and designed the chassis which carried them to several World Championships in road-racing. Joep Broekmans did the development work on the chassis and the unit was found to be ideal. The design is a broad Duplex cradle which is quite close to the engine all round, with the motor itself being an important bracing member. As the engine is quite wide at its base, the frame naturally splays out around it, thus giving the machine a bulky look.

'The engine goes this way', the Citroën-based unit fitted into the frame.

Front suspension is by Koni gas dampers, while Koni gas units attach the aluminium swinging arm on the left and the shaft drive on the right to the frame. Cast-iron Brembo discs are used, in the usual twin front and single rear pattern. Apart from the engine, the bike looks very conventional but this does not hide the impeccable finish of the machine. Although standard Honda switchgear is used, VDO were commissioned to produce the instruments and came up with a three-dial display of 260 kph speedometer, and 9,000 rpm tachometer flanking a petrol gauge. All the instruments are of green background with white numerals and dayglo orange needles. To accompany these, are warning lights for just about everything, including water temperature, oil pressure and brake failure. The only complaint about the controls is the archaic positioning of the ignition under the tank and just behind the large cooling radiator. The last Van Veen made featured a superbly stylish fairing and this incorporated re-mounted instruments and a replaced ignition, but unfortunately this was just to be a one-off.

Weighing a gargantuan 642 lb, the Van Veen OCR1000 makes no pretensions that it is anything other than a very large bike and the absence of a side stand makes this all the more noticeable when first you try to push it off the huge centre unit. The suspension catches the bike as it hits the deck and you are immediately aware that it has a very well damped chassis indeed. With the ignition on, the starter motor eases the Wankel into life and, for those with no experience of such an engine, the disappointment will soon set in. Those who think that the rotary engine is as smooth as silk will be disenchanted, for the growl exuding from the two sculptured exhaust pipes sounds like a cross between an unsilenced four-cylinder four-stroke and a graunchy two-stroke bike. There is little vibration, however, but the motor still feels harsh. A quick blip of the throttle produces an instant response and the faster the engine turns over (if such an expression can correctly be used for a Wankel), the smoother it feels. Just like the little Hercules/DKW W2000 with its snowmobile engine of the same design, the Van Veen is eager for revs and somehow seems restrained by a mediocre rev limit of 6,500 rpm.

Although the gearbox isn't as smooth as those of several Japanese bikes, it doesn't baulk too badly and the clutch is a pure delight. Naturally, with just

If ever there was a bike engineered down to the last nut and bolt it was the Van Veen, with its sculptured exhausts and specially cast wheels.

four gears, the overall gearing is going to be on the high side, but the motor just takes the long-legged first gear and surges the machine forward with remarkable force and smoothness. Changing ratios is quite a tricky practice with a combination of shaft drive and Wankel engine, and a missed gear down the box will result in a whole bagful of revs past the red line and an obvious chirp from the rear tyre as it locks when the unsynchronised change is finally made. A lot of practice is needed but that will reward the rider who takes a little time and exercises a little care. When the bike was announced in 1976, the company claimed a top speed of just a shade under 150 mph, but common sense now prevails and it is obvious that a Honda CBX with around

80 lb less to carry and 5 bhp more, and a top speed of 138-140 mph, will make the OCR seem a little slower. Not very many people could cope with such performance and such a high seating position and high handlebars. A genuine top speed of 122 mph can be obtained while acceleration over ¼ mile from a standing start shouldn't occupy much more than 12.5 sec.

The handling and roadholding of the Van Veen are excellent for such a big bike with the Pirelli endurance racing tyres mounted on the Campagnolo wheels gripping the bike to the road in all weathers. The whole plot is very tidy in corners although naturally it doesn't have the racer-like responses of the racing Kriedlers! Quite large angles of lean can be obtained but all of a sudden raising the bike back to vertical gets tiresome and the machine's sheer bulk soon tells.

The biggest drawback of the bike is fuel consumption which ranges between a frugal 32 mpg on the lightest of throttles to a wallet-emptying 20 mpg which soon drains the 4.75 gal tank as well. It is hard to ride such a revvy engine with tight reins, too.

At a price of around £5,500, even back in 1977, it was obvious that just a few buyers would have the cash or need for such a unique bike. The idea was

right and the design was superb with just about the best of all worlds, but such a painstakingly constructed machine as the Van Veen OCR1000 would be of little else except novelty value to most people. It came as little surprise when in 1978, Henk Van Veen decided that his venture would be able to go no further.

Engine: Comotor transversely mounted, twin-rotor Wankel of 996cc. Single 32 mm carburettor. Maximum power 100 bhp at 6,000 rpm. Electric start.

Transmission: dry twin-disc clutch and four-speed gearbox. Shaft final drive.

Frame and suspension: Duplex cradle and telescopic fork with rear swinging arm and coil-spring/damper units.

Brakes: twin discs front and single disc rear.

Performance: maximum speed 122 mph, acceleration over a standing start ¼ mile 12.5 sec. Fuel consumption 30 mpg.

The instruments of the Van Veen are aimed squarely at the rider.

HONDA CBX

After the launch of the CB750 in 1968, Honda seemed to stay out of the limelight as bigger and faster machines were marketed by the opposition, notably Kawasaki. With the introduction of the touring Gold Wing, with its 1-litre flat-four, there seemed to be little on offer for the sports enthusiasts either. Surely Honda wouldn't pare weight off the shaft-drive monster and offer it as their answer to the Z900. No, indeed they didn't, but customers longing for a sports bike with a 1-litre engine had to wait some time before the company came up with the goods. In 1976, it was decided that Honda should create the fastest motorcycle in production anywhere and, with a healthy team of four-stroke bikes doing so well in endurance racing, that seemed to be the obvious place to start. Two designs were contemplated, one a four and the other a six. Both would use four-valve heads and both should produce the best part of 100 bhp. After 6 months of development, the six was chosen because it had a

little more power, had smoother delivery of power and, of course, it *was* a six, and whatever it was it would sell itself if it sported that many cylinders. Soichiro Irimajiri headed the design team and his credentials were as good as anybody's, for he was also responsible for the incredible range of racers that Honda fielded in the 1960s, including the 250cc six and the 125cc five.

The CBX uses a 1,047cc engine of oversquare dimensions mounted across the frame. Breathing is through two banks of three 28 mm Keihin carburettors which are set on manifolds angling backwards from the centre so that they don't protrude outside the fuel tank. The head design of the bike is quite

That superb engine is super-sensitive to the throttle and never ceases to amaze the rider with the power and smoothness which go hand-in-hand.

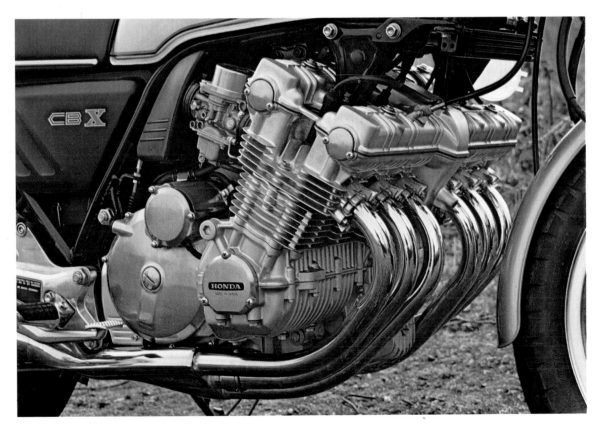

complex, with one Hy-Vo chain driving the exhaust camshaft and another chain driving the inlet cam from that. The cams actuate four valves per cylinder which makes twenty-four in all, and is obviously quite a nightmare for maintenance work. With a 9.3:1 compression ratio, the engine produces 105 bhp at 9,000 rpm and a healthy maximum torque of 62.2 lb ft at 8,000 rpm; the motor thrives on revs and has a red line at 9,500 rpm, quite astonishing for such a large engine. Masahuri Tsuboi overcame the problem of engine width by placing the alternator behind the cylinders and driving it from the crankshaft by chain and jackshaft. Usually, the unit is bolted on to the end of the crank where it is not so much of a hindrance on smaller power units. In fact, across the block, the CBX engine is little wider than a four, although naturally it is much larger around the cylinder head. Another problem with a six is flexing of the crankshaft, and this has been remedied by having the power take-off point in between the two central cylinders. Drive is taken through a wet multi-plate clutch and five-speed gearbox and then to a conventional chain final drive.

More racing design was applied to the CBX in the frame, for, just like the earlier racers, Irimajiri used a broad diamond-type frame from which to hang the engine rather than insert it into a conventional Duplex type. It works quite well, but without conventional downtubes the bike has a weird naked appearance from the front. Normal forks and swinging arm suspensions are used, however.

Unquestionably, the CBX is a large bike and feels even bigger once you are perched on the 32 in saddle and look down to see nothing but engine beneath. Somehow the weight has been kept down to 548 lb with the engine making up a quite trifling 233 lb of that. The engine will usually fire first time, whatever the weather, and ticks over smoothly and with no vibration to speak of. The exhaust note from the twin tailpipes is quite reminiscent of a four and is nowhere near as delightful as the six-throated whine of the Benelli 750. Maybe the company wanted a subdued note for the engine, but the twin pipes do 'cut' the line of the bike in a way as to make

The Honda CBX is Honda high technology gone mad, with its hollow camshafts for weight-saving and its multiplicity of valves.

The high bars of the CBX make the rider feel like a sail to the wind. The extra wind drag matters not a bit to the engine, however.

it look smaller from a distance. The way that the engine responds to the throttle is amazing, and it is hard to avoid clichés likening it to gas turbine engines and the like.

The CBX is every inch a road-burner and one has great difficulty in holding back when the road is clear. Acceleration away from a standstill is amazing with ¼ mile being reached in just on 11.5 sec. That alone cannot tell how it gets there for it just lifts up its skirts and rockets away, and the bike needs little provocation to get the front wheel pawing at the air. It is one thing popping wheelies on RD400 Yamahas and equivalent middleweights, but getting

take-off on a six-cylinder 548 lb heavyweight is another matter. Riding in town can be a nightmare, and that has nothing to do with the size or docility of the machine; when a quick glimpse is taken of the speedometer, often you are travelling 20-30 mph quicker than you had planned, and that is bad news if there are any police, pedestrians or errant unsuspecting cars lurking. Top speed is hampered by the large frontal area offered to the wind, but with conditions just right it might be possible to squeeze an honest 140 mph out of the bike.

With such easy performance on tap, fuel consumption can be a little heavy and it is quite a simple matter to return less than 30 mpg. Even with careful riding, you cannot reasonably expect more than 35 mpg, but a 5.28 gal tank should help make long journeys less of a fuel-filling chore.

For such a large bike, the Honda handles remarkably well and is rarely upset on smooth roads. When there is a rippling or bumpy surface to contend with, however, the bike becomes more of a handful and a great deal of wariness is demanded. In recent years, Japanese frames have become more respectable and not the articulated-feeling affairs that once graced that country's motorcycles. Obviously, a lot of racing know-how has gone into the CBX racing-type frame and all the criticisms can be aimed at the spring/damper units rather than at any lack of rigidity of the chassis.

Braking is taken care of by two 11 in discs at the front and a 12 in unit at the rear which are quite adequate in use in the dry, although they show the typical stainless steel trait of being ponderous in the wet.

Aircraft-style instruments are used and they are among the best to be found on any bike, featuring two large dials for the speedometer and tachometer with dayglo orange markings on a black background. In between is a voltmeter, where a fuel gauge would have been more handy. Where the CBX differs greatly from other bikes is in the handlebars; in fact, it doesn't have one bar but two, just like the clip-ons used on café racers. However, the bars are in the more usual upright position rather than placed so as to encourage a racing-style crouch. One neat touch is the fitting of little round nuts on the edge of the footpegs which gently graze the road surface when the bike is cornered hard. These give adequate warning of the cornering angle and are necessary as there is precious little else to

The rev counter is redlined at 9,500 rpm and there is a legend emblazoned on the fuel tank stating roughly how many pieces will get into orbit should that limit be overstepped by an appreciable amount.

scrape and warn the rider of the degree of bank.

Since the CBX was announced, Kawasaki have brought out their six and, in the last stages of development, upped its capacity by 100cc to try to give it the performance edge over the lighter Honda. However, in a back-to-back test, the air-cooled machine wins out over its water-cooled rival because it still has that biting power only a four-valve engine can produce. The Z1300 may be able to beat it accelerating from low speeds in high gears but the CBX rules the roost on the dragstrips. With a much-

rumoured vee-six water-cooled shaft-drive six on the cards, the CBX took everyone by surprise when it was launched. It may have been that Honda, before releasing a complete new range of bikes, wanted to show the world just how much they had learned from their endurance racing bikes. In terms of sheer power and speed, they have proved just that and, to save wasting valuable development time on a bike that was shelved, the company recently lowered the capacity of their 1-litre four, which ran alongside the six in development, and offered it as the 95 bhp CBFZ900.

Engine: transversely mounted, six-cylinder four-stroke of 1,047cc with four valves per cylinder operated by twin overhead camshafts. Six 28 mm carburettors. Maximum power 105 bhp at 9,000 rpm. Electric start.

Transmission: wet multi-plate clutch and five-speed gearbox. Chain final drive.

Frame and suspension: backbone diamond frame with telescopic front fork and rear swinging arm with coil-spring/damper units.

Brakes: twin discs front and single disc rear.

Performance: maximum speed 140 mph, acceleration over a standing start ¼ mile 11.5 sec. Fuel consumption 35 mpg.

YAMAHA XS1100

For many years, Yamaha were completely out of the superbike race as the largest machine they had on offer in most markets was a 650 cc twin. That was changed when they brought out their XS750 which started several new trends, not least being the adoption of shaft drive on an across-the-frame multi-cylinder bike. Yamaha attracted many sales with their 750 and the machine's only major criticism was that it was a little underpowered. All that changed, however, when the company took the step of building their next up-market bike which turned out to be the XS1100, at the time the biggest thing on two wheels apart from the Harley-Davidsons.

The basic layout of the XS1100 is similar to the 750 with the notable exception being that the larger bike has one more cylinder, making it four instead of a 120° triple. The 750's stroke of 68.6 mm was retained, but the bore was increased from 68 to 71.5 mm, making a swept volume of 1,102 cc. Breathing through four 34 mm constant vacuum Mikuni carburettors, the engine produces 95 bhp at 8,000 rpm and a peak torque figure of 66.5 lb ft at 6,500 rpm. That is only part of the story of the power output, however, for the engine's torque curve is remarkably flat with around 60 lb ft of torque being developed from 3,000 rpm. As well as being impressive on paper, that makes for smooth acceleration and lots of it. A Hy-Vo chain takes the power from the centre of the crankshaft and drives *via* a wet multi-plate clutch to a five-speed gearbox and thence to a shaft drive running down the left-hand side of the bike.

The engine/transmission is housed in a conventional Duplex frame which appears to be very rigid. Unlike other superbikes, the Yamaha chassis offers no tricks and is very much an orthodox design. Three 11.73 in discs are fitted and are of stainless steel.

Weighing almost 600 lb dry, and with a seat height of 32 in, the XS1100 looks an imposing machine and, when at first you are seated in the generous saddle, that impression stays as the bike feels quite enormous. Once off the centre stand, however, the feeling is negated just a little and the

The mighty Yamaha XS1100 is a tourer with the sort of low-down power which almost makes the gearbox redundant.

conventional sequence is carried through for starting the bike: ignition on and press the button. One must remember first to unlock the steering fork lock under the steering head because the big Yamaha also has a lock in the ignition and it is quite easy to insert the key and release one while still forgetting the other. Whether having a second more conventional lock is of any use is debatable for, if one swift turn of the bars can break one, surely it can quite easily break two.

Somehow, the engine doesn't feel quite as smooth as most other Japanese fours and definitely the gear change is a little more vague than most of its competitors; this is due to a fairly long pedal linkage, as well as the obvious problems with shaft drive. Acceleration is quite superb, with 95 bhp to play with, but again, because of the bike's height and bulk, getting away from standstill briskly takes a lot of practice and a fair bit of nerve. The weight seems to be of little importance once under way, and

Everything about the XS is excess in size but its followers, who wax lyrical about its cross-continent abilities, are many.

with natural balance restored, and the Yamaha races up to its 8,500 rpm red line in the lower gears. A standing start ¼ mile can take just under 12 sec, while a top speed of around 135 mph can be expected. Fuel consumption is excellent for a large bike and one can expect 45 mpg on long touring rides, with the figure only seriously falling below 38 mpg when all the performance is used all of the time. As is sometimes the case with such powerful motorcycles, lots of use around town can confuse the rider and occasionally one forgets exactly what gear is engaged. There is so much pull from so low down the rev range that winding the throttle open in most ratios will leave most traffic for dead.

Cornering at slow speeds takes getting used to

The drive side of the big Yamaha showing the final shaft and the complex gearchange mechanism.

Whatever way you look at it, the XS1100 is a big bike and it certainly needs a strong rider to handle it around town.

with the XS1100, for it tends to oversteer into tight corners; in other words it seems to fall into them. This can be quite frightening when it first happens and, of course, can be made all the worse when it is raining. Once you reach about 15-20 mph though, the bike feels a lot steadier and the upright riding position helps give confidence when using a lot of steering lock. Traffic can be negotiated with relative ease and the smooth power take up is also an advantage.

Cornering at fairly high speeds is quite adequate, but when you start to use all the power further up the speed range, then there are several habits displayed that are not too nice. The roles are reversed when you start charging into and out of corners, for once again the weight seems to be against you as it pulls you into bends. The manners are fairly reasonable as long as a steady throttle opening is kept and as long as just one line is used. Slow down, accelerate or tighten a line in a corner and the balance will be upset, while trying to accelerate hard too early from a bend will show up a traction problem, even with a massive 4.5 in wide rear tyre between the bike and the road. No, the big 'Yam' makes no pretences at being a sports machine and is much better suited to long-legged touring where its engine will pull two people and luggage along for mile after easy mile at three-figure speeds.

A firm grip has to made on the lever to get the twin front discs into quick action and a lot of effort has to be exerted to haul so much weight down from high speed. In the wet, a great deal of caution has to be taken, for there is a long delay before the pads start to work on the soaked discs and then they tend to grab a little. The calipers for the front wheel are located under the forks, and it has been said that water tends to get thrown in a torrent into brakes so placed, when they would be less affected above and in front of the forks.

At a quick glance, before you count the cylinders, the XS1100 is distinguished from its smaller stablemate by the oblong headlight which, in practice, is very efficient indeed. To complement the angled light is a set of square instruments with a 160 mph

The unique instrumentation of the Yamaha and the excellent switchgear allow the rider to concentrate fully on the task at hand.

would be a good option to offer the European buyers. Two designers were commissioned, David Weightmann and John Mockett, and they teamed up with sculptor Steve Furlonger and aerodynamicist Barry Hobson to produce a two-part body. The upper portion turns with the handlebars and so doesn't hinder the steering lock, while the lower section provides leg protection for the rider, as well as an aerodynamic aid at high speed. Made of glass fibre, the fairing is sturdy enough to carry the headlight and indicators of the naked bike, along with two recessed driving or fog lights, one either side.

Engine: transversely mounted, four-cylinder four-stroke of 1,102cc with two valves per cylinder operated by twin overhead camshafts. Four 34 mm carburettors. Maximum power 95 bhp at 8,000 rpm. Electric start.

Transmission: wet multi-plate clutch and five-speed gearbox. Shaft final drive.

Frame and suspension: Duplex cradle with telescopic front fork and rear swinging arm with coil-spring/damper units.

Brakes: twin discs front and single disc rear.

Performance: maximum speed 135 mph, acceleration over a standing start ¼ mile 11.9 sec. Fuel consumption 40 mpg.

speedometer to the left of the tachometer, which also houses a handy fuel gauge. Fuel stops need not be that frequent, however, for the Yamaha sports a massive 5.28 gal fuel tank, which gives somewhere between 200 and 250 miles between fillings.

Also fitted as standard are self-cancelling indicators and a very handy cutout device which will kill the engine should the bike fall over. This of course cuts the chances of a fire and of serious engine damage which has been known when a bike has fallen onto its twistgrip, thus opening the throttle and subsequently the cylinders to the world.

With such an able tourer as the Yamaha XS1100 in production, the company decided that a fairing

KAWASAKI Z1300

During the early 1970s, Kawasaki enjoyed (and encouraged!) a reputation for machines that were fast and furious. Indeed, the Z900 and Z1000 models proved so popular that they came to be known as 'The King' by motorcycle enthusiasts. As time passed, however, the King came to be dethroned by a host of rival machines that were faster and even more powerful. It was time for Kawasaki to hit back and, at the Cologne Motor Cycle Show in 1978, they unveiled their new heavyweight contender, the Z1300. The bike created an immediate sensation. It stopped even the most blasé motorcycling journalists dead in their tracks; reducing everyone who set eyes on it to a look of open-mouthed incredulity.

The Z1300 was more than just an attempt by Kawasaki to put itself back on top of the high-performance tree. It was a statement to its rivals that 'anything you can do we can do better' — or, at least, bigger! The bike absolutely bristled with technical innovations. It was as though Kawasaki

had taken every technical innovation pioneered by the Japanese industry and incorporated it into a single machine. At first it seemed as though the Z1300 had been aimed mainly at the technical journalist rather than members of the motorcycling public. Indeed, the Z1300's technical specification reads like an advertising copywriter's dream. As a monument to Japanese technical overkill the Z1300 stands alone.

The power unit of the Z1300 is a 1,286cc, in-line, six-cylinder motor fitted with twin overhead camshafts and three double-choke 32 mm Mikuni carburettors. The claimed power output is a staggering 120 bhp at 8,000 rpm, making the Z1300 the most powerful mass-production motorcycle ever built. At 85.4 lb ft, the Z1300 certainly doesn't lack

The big Kawasaki is water-cooled so that the cylinders can be closer to each other, thus saving a little in width.

Sintered steel brake pads and drilled discs enable the Z1300 to stop well in all weathers.

The Kawasaki Z1300 is the biggest of the bunch of production bikes and has the most power.

for torque either. Not content with designing the world's largest six-cylinder motorcycle engine, Kawasaki went one step further and gave it water-cooling. This, they argued, would allow them to place the cylinders closer together, thus enabling them to keep engine width to a minimum. It would also help to keep the engine cooler and allow the engine to run more smoothly. By placing a large water radiator at the front of the engine, however, Kawasaki unfortunately managed to reduce the visual impact that a 'naked' six-cylinder unit might have had. Kawasaki also had a problem in that a six-pipe exhaust system would have taken up too much space. Consequently they settled for a six-into-two pipe system which further disguised the engine's six cylinders.

The engine is not the only item likely to catch the eye of the technically minded motorcyclist. Disc brakes are fitted front and rear and feature sintered disc brake pads, a great step forward in the fight against poor wet-weather braking. The transmission too is interesting in that the bike is shaft driven, thus eliminating the need to replace chains at alarmingly frequent intervals. In fact, the Z1300 boasts a whole host of innovations, many of which go totally unnoticed at first. For example, the Z1300 has a steering lock which is operated from the ignition key. Even more cunning is the electrical cut-out switch hidden away in the side cover. This little device could leave many would-be thieves scratching their heads in puzzlement as they discover their traditional 'hot wiring' methods are no longer working.

Apart from its technical specifications, the Z1300 is an imposing machine in its own right. It is huge; there is no other word for it. It stands 32 in high at saddle height, has a wheelbase of 62.48 in and weighs a colossal 710 lb. The impression of obesity is not helped either by the fact that the huge 5.6 gal fuel tank is slab-shaped and painted an uninspiring dark bluey-green colour. The saddle seems big enough for three people, let alone one, and the handlebars are set high and wide. Parked at the kerbside, fully fuelled and ready to run, the Z1300 presents a daunting sight to the in-experienced rider.

Surprisingly, however, once the bike is on the move, it proves much more manoeuvrable than its bulk might initially suggest. The engine is incredibly smooth and there is no noticeable power

Clear instrumentation is a strong point on the Z1300.

band. The power simply feeds in at low revs and keeps coming until the rider either runs out of road or nerve. To achieve this smoothness, Kawasaki have fitted what they call a 'harmonic damper' to the big machine's crankshaft. The damper's duty is to absorb the crank's torsional impulses, turning the excess energy into heat which is then dissipated.

The shaft-drive system too is instrumental in adding to the overall smoothness of the bike. The shaft eliminates the whiplash effect of chain snatch that so plagues normal large-capacity chain-driven motorcycles. The fact that the shaft is so smooth is largely due to four separate couplers of one kind or another that have been interposed between the

A shaft is used for final drive — I am sure the Kawasaki engineers wondered about the sanity of transmitting 120 bhp by chain on such a heavy bike.

Z1300's crankshaft and the rear wheel hub. In addition, the five-speed gearbox is a pleasure to use, with almost none of the grinding and clunking normally associated with shaft-driven machines. It certainly is superior in action to that of a BMW, for so long the epitome of the shaft-driven tourer.

Clutch action on the Z1300 is also light and smooth and, even in heavy traffic, the bike is most pleasant to ride; which is just as well because the sheer size and weight of the beast makes it a real handful to manoeuvre in tight situations. The centre stand is sensibly placed and relatively easy to operate but, once off the stand, the only thing preventing the bike from toppling to the ground is the strength of the rider. Needless to say, 90 lb weaklings, needn't apply for Z1300 ownership. On the move, however, the size of the bike seems to diminish. It is still noticeably heavier than most machines, however, although the smoothness of the engine and transmission does much to disguise the fact.

Opening the throttle quickly on the Z1300 produces some interesting results. With 120 bhp on tap, the bike launches itself forward in a most impressive manner, shrugging off the excess weight with an air of contempt. The rear suspension seems to give a heave, hunches itself down and, with a groan, the bike gallops off down the road like a bull elephant on the rampage. A standing ¼ mile can be

disposed of in 12.5 sec while the magic 100 mph mark arrives in a shade over 10 sec. For a bike that is at its best as a two-up tourer that kind of performance is not to be sneered at. True, the Z1300 is not as fast as its lighter Japanese six-cylinder rival, the Honda CBX1000, but it does 'at least return an overall fuel consumption of 42 mpg, a 10 mpg improvement over its smaller and lighter rival.

The Kawasaki Z1300 may well prove to be the end of an era. The present day energy crisis will make the justification of bikes like the Z1300 more and more difficult. It simply is too excessive to fit the market requirements of today's motorcycling society; which is a pity because, for all its shortcomings, the Z1300 is an incredible motorcycle to ride and a tribute to the technological ability of the design staff at Kawasaki in Japan.

Engine: transversely mounted, six-cylinder four-stroke of 1,286cc with two valves per cylinder operated by twin overhead camshafts. Three twin-choke 32 mm carburettors. Maximum power 120 bhp at 8,000 rpm. Electric start.

Transmission: wet multi-plate clutch and five-speed gearbox. Shaft final drive.

Frame and suspension: Duplex cradle with telescopic front fork and rear swinging arm with coil-spring/damper units.

Brakes: twin discs front and single disc rear.

Performance: maximum speed 136 mph, acceleration over a standing start ¼ mile 12.3 sec. Fuel consumption 42 mpg.

MÜNCH MAMMUT

There are countless problems awaiting a small manufacturer when he decides to produce a new motorcycle, even though the cycle part itself is fairly easy for accomplished engineers. It is the motor part which is the most difficult to manufacture, especially if our hypothetical constructor wants to break into the multi-cylinder world of the superbikes. Rickman, Seeley and Bimota produce their machines, but it involves buying either a complete Suzuki, Kawasaki or Honda, taking out the engine and thus wasting the best part of the rest of the bike. Throughout the history of the motorcycle, however, there have been engineers who have cleared this hurdle by using a different approach: building cycles to accommodate car engines. Car units are cheap, easy to obtain and usually have the required amount of cylinders for your average superbike.

In 1932, George Brough fitted an 800cc Austin four into a sidecar outfit, while, on the other side of the Atlantic, people have been fitting automobile engines into bike frames right from the early days when it wasn't uncommon to see even V8 motors nestling within the confines of a Duplex frame. More recently, Drac Moto of Barcelona have marketed their Shifty which features a water-cooled Fiat four-cylinder engine of 900cc, but so far the most successful machine produced on these lines is the Mammut built by Friedel Münch.

Münch was a motorcycle dealer who lived in Ossenheim in the Hessen Hills of Germany and who devoted a great deal of time to tuning and repairing Horex machines. In the early 1960s, Jean Murit, himself a bike dealer from Paris and one time racer, dropped by and asked whether Münch could construct for him a 120 mph road bike . . . at whatever cost. Having had a similar idea in his mind at the time, Münch agreed and quickly constructed this bike using an NSU Prinz car engine. *Das Motorrad* journalist, Ernst Leverkus, found out about the project and insisted that he would be the first to try the bike, and this was agreed. In the first trials, it was obvious that the performance parameters laid down in the basic specification could be met with ease, and it wasn't long before

The Münch Mammut is now probably just like its namesake, extinct, but who knows what the future may hold?

Münch found that his secret was out and that offers were coming in from most parts of the world.

Obviously, full-scale production which would rock the Japanese was out of the question but soon, as the late 1960s came and drifted into the '70s, a steady one to one and a half bikes were being assembled each week. As the production was so steady, various detail improvements could be incorporated in each new model which left the works.

Before Münch decided to give up the Mammut project in 1979, after various financial bothers and mis-dealings with various financiers, to set up the Horex name again building turbo bikes, the machines he produced were a world apart from the early brutal-looking and performing monsters that had lived up well to the 'Mammoth' title. They looked neater and more like conventional bikes, and handled and performed exceptionally well. The 1977 machines were designated 1300 TTS/E, the number for the capacity, TTS from the NSU engine used, and the E for the electronic fuel injection fitted to give them that extra pep.

The TTS engine is an air-cooled parallel four as mounted in the rear of the NSU, but here fitted transversely across the Mammut frame. Of alloy construction, the engine sits high in the frame and its major drawback is that the engine is quite tall itself so that there is little clearance below the tank. Drive is taken from the left side of the crankshaft upwards to the single overhead camshaft which actuates two valves per cylinder *via* rockers; from the other end of the engine, drive is taken by gear to the transmission. When the NSU engines are stripped at the factory, the bore is increased from standard so that the heavily oversquare unit displaces 1,287cc. Breathing through Kugelfischer fuel injection, the engine produces a healthy 104 bhp at 7,500 rpm. The NSU oil-cooler is dispensed with and the lubricating fluid is pumped through twin units either side of the frame just under the steering head. A magnesium sump is fitted also to increase the capacity, reduce the weight and aid cooling.

The power is taken from the primary drive through a dry multi-plate clutch and thence to a positive-stop four-speed gearbox developed from the unit used in the Horex Imperator of the late 1950s. With so much torque on hand, only four gears are really necessary, and the only obvious sign of the

gearbox's age is that its change pattern is reversed, with one up and three down. Final drive is transferred from the right side of the bike back to the left where it goes through a chain drive fully enclosed in its own oil bath to the back wheel. Early machines were prone to eating their chains, but the 1977 bikes cope well, their items being of Japanese DID manufacture.

The frame of the bike can readily show its origins as being based on the legendary 'Featherbed' Norton unit, and the design features the same faintly rectangular narrow Duplex design. On the early bikes, front forks were by Münch and then Rickman units were fitted. After another brief time on Cerianis, the last machines ended up with what

Twin Weber carburettors feed this unit's engine, as ever of NSU manufacture.

rider yet still almost behind the trailing edge of the rear wheel. The compromise was changed on the last bikes with the fitting of a single saddle and racing-style support. A massive 5.5 gal tank separates the rider from the low clip-on-style bars and the indentations in the tank are very necessary for the rider to place his knees comfortably. Keeping the wind off the rider is a Rickman nose fairing, inside which are three extra instruments: an oil-pressure gauge, voltmeter and clock.

A Bosch starter motor gets the bike into life and the NSU engine growls menacingly into its four-into-two exhaust. The clutch is relatively light, but the gear change is awkward and vague but sooner or later engages into the correct ratio. Once off the tall centre stand, the bike feels quite a handful, bearing in mind that crouched forward the rider has to balance the best part of 600 lb worth of expensive bike. Once rolling, however, the Münch is quite easy to control and doesn't oversteer at all as one would expect of a large bike. The engine is kept smooth by the superb injection and pulls from low speed with no fuss or fluffing of plugs. Gear changing is tedious and the best plan of action is to get into the highest gear and let the engine do the work of a deft left foot. Once under way, the bike fairly rushes forward and can reach 60 mph in just a shade over 4 sec and then on to ¼ mile time from standing start in 12.6 sec. Top speed is governed by the gearing, with 126 mph coming up easily at the red line. Unless the Münch is hammered, fuel

should have been fitted in the first place: Marzocchi units. Likewise, the rear end, which started with Girling, went on to the efficient Konis but ended with expensive Corte & Cosso gas units. Triple cross-drilled cast-iron Brembo discs are fitted and neat Campagnolo alloy wheels complete the rolling chassis specification.

With a large transmission and enormous inlet tracts for the injection, the engine indeed takes up a great deal of space in the long frame and there is precious little room for the rider. Early bikes had twin saddles with the passenger cramped behind the

Believe it or not, there is actually a chain in that metal casing for the final drive.

consumption is quite frugal with 40 mpg possible with a gentle rider. Even pressed hard, the consumption should stay around 29-30 mpg, which is fair for such a powerful bike.

With a stout frame and sturdy swinging arm, along with the excellent Marzocchi forks, handling even at speed is good, with no wallowing and no apparent chassis flex. Ultimate grip of course depends on what tyres are specified, but the sheer bulk of the bike crosses the rider's mind long before the pilot gets any ideas about taking it to its limits. Indeed, the centre stand, which hangs down a long way, just around the front of the back wheel, is a handy thing to have to let you know when something is scraping the tarmac.

Since Friedel Münch left the concern, there have been no more bikes and he is now starting up a new project, producing his own single-cylinder machines of up to 750cc under the Horex banner. Also, he is upping the performance of several of his old Münch bikes for customers who need (or think they need!) 1,400 or 1,600cc machines. If this is not enough, the man will supply you with (type approval permitting) his 1,400cc turbo Horex. It produces 140 bhp, tops 150 mph and no doubt will be that little something for the motorcyclist who has (or thinks he has) everything!

Engine: NSU transversely mounted, four-cylinder four-stroke of 1,287cc with two valves per cylinder operated, *via* rockers, by a single overhead camshaft. Fuel injection. Maximum power 104 bhp at 7,500 rpm. Electric start.

Transmission: dry multi-plate clutch and four-speed gearbox. Chain final drive.

Frame and suspension: Duplex cradle with telescopic front fork and rear swinging arm with coil-spring/damper units.

Brakes: twin discs front and single disc rear.

Performance: maximum speed 126 mph, acceleration over a standing start ¼ mile 12.6 sec. Fuel consumption 30 mpg.

This older Mammut model features drum brakes at either end which were not really up to the task of stopping the bike without abnormal fade.

INDEX

ACKNOWLEDGEMENTS

The author would like to thank the following for their invaluable help and advice:
  Clive Gorman, Mike Maxwell, Barry Winfield, Mike Winfield.

Additional illustrations were supplied by:
  Jan Heese, Rickman Group of Companies, Colin Seeley International, Superbike.

Motorcycles were supplied by:
  Harold Coppock Racing, Brize Norton, Oxon, US (Suzuki RG500 Mk IV); Fowlers of Bristol, UK (Yamaha TZ750); Honda (GB) Ltd, Chiswick, London, UK (Honda Endurance Racer, Honda MT125R); Kawasaki (UK) Ltd, Slough, Bucks, UK (Kawasaki KR250); Loder's Motorcycles, Dorchester, Dorset, UK (BMW R100RS, Honda Goldwing); Motorcycle City Ltd, Farnborough, Hants, UK (Suzuki GS1000S, Laverda Jota, Triumph Bonneville, Honda CBX, Honda XL500S, Yamaha XS1100, Suzuki SP370/400); Superbiking, Station Garage, Taplow, Bucks, UK (Kawasaki Z1000ST, Kawasaki Z1300, MV-Agusta Monza, Benelli 900/6); Three Cross Motorcycles, Verwood, Dorset, UK (Moto-Guzzi 850, Le Mans Mk II, Ducati 900SS, Ducati Hailwood Replica, Harley-Davidson XLCR 1000).